S.A.I.N.T.

How to live more fully in the Spirit

Charles Jacquin

BALBOA.
PRESS

A DIVISION OF HAY HOUSE

Balboa Press books may be ordered through booksellers or by contacting:

Balboa Press
A Division of Hay House
1663 Liberty Drive
Bloomington, IN 47403
www.balboapress.com
1 (877) 407-4847

Printed in the United States of America.

ISBN: 978-1-4525-8412-6 (sc)
ISBN: 978-1-4525-8413-3 (e)

Library of Congress Control Number: 2013918208

Balboa Press rev. date: 11/12/2013

CONTENTS

DEDICATION

For Sam.

PREFACE

S.A.I.N.T. is about discovering or increasing your awareness of how to live more fully in the spirit. Through the practice of S.A.I.N.T. you will discover the richness of God in your daily life.

S.A.I.N.T. illustrates experience of the Divine through personal stories. The author explains how each of us is capable of developing and demonstrating the behavior and lifestyle of a saint. The simplicity of the S.A.I.N.T. practice will enable you to better understand yourself and others whom you meet. The fog of uncertainty and doubt of life's circumstances will be lifted from you. Simply open yourself up to the energy of Spirit and the mundane becomes extraordinary.

INTRODUCTION

"**I** am a saint!"
Close your eyes and silently repeat this phrase to yourself. "I am a saint." How does this feel? Is it real to you?

The goal of this book is for you to be able to say these words and know in the depth of your being that they are true. "But . . . of course, I'm not a saint," you may say to yourself. "I'm no Mother Theresa, that's for sure!" Like most people, you may believe that "sainthood" is for a special few who have passed a process of beatification by church authorities. This is not the kind of sainthood I'm talking about. I'm talking about a lifestyle, a way of functioning in this world. Sainthood is actually a simple and natural state of being . . . if you are willing to grow and sustain faith in heavenly standards beyond those of your own.

In this book you will read many of my personal stories and philosophies, but *you* are the real focus of this book. This book exists for you—to serve your growth in whatever way that it can. I do talk about my own journey, because that is what I know. I hope you will benefit from whatever I have learned and gain faith from the miracles that I have observed along my path. But *your* miracles and *your* journey are the real story.

My hope is that this book will both challenge you and bring ease to your spiritual journey. I intend to give you tools to use, but I also hope to shake you out of the sleep of spiritual complacency, the kind that puts God in a small box and limits your experience of divinity to church buildings and spiritual gatherings. Theoretically, we have all been taught that God is omnipresent in the world, but rarely do we live as though this simple idea—that God is everywhere—is actually real in our three-dimensional world. Rarely do we live as though God is right here in the midst of us at a board meeting at work. Rarely do we consider that the Holy Spirit is present when we say "hello" to an acquaintance at the grocery store. And of course we forget all about Him when we are feeling tired, anxious, or annoyed.

I hope to illustrate to you that miracles can happen when you allow the reality of God's continuous presence in your life. And I encourage you to realize how amazingly simple and natural it is to be a bona fide saint in this world. Miracles do not require supernatural ability. Rather, miracles are a matter of opening yourself to the experience of the Holy Spirit and allowing Him to flow through you unimpeded. There are no special credentials required to make this happen; you merely open up and let love flow through you. And in the process, you discover depth and richness in your relationship with God as you have never experienced it before.

Throughout this book, I use Christian terminology and only occasionally reference other religions and spiritual practices. I do this simply because this is what I know, and it is the message and imagery that personally resonates with me. Please know, however, that this book is not about theology. It is a practice that can be used by anyone of any persuasion. I am encouraging everyone to strive to be a saint in his or her own time. What a wonderful world this would be if it were full of Christian saints, or Buddhist saints, Hindu saints, Jewish saints, Muslim saints or any kind of saint imaginable!

The gift of miracles is part of the official standard of saintliness, a requirement to be recognized as a saint by the Roman Catholic Church. Perhaps my definition of "saint" is a little bit different from official church doctrine. Miracles do happen for saints, though I'm not sure that quality is actually necessary. What we call a "miracle" involves external happenings, while true saintliness is an internal state of being. Nevertheless, I do believe that you will experience miracles just as I have. You will observe amazing synchronicities and will watch as complex human problems resolve themselves before your eyes. These shifts in reality are nothing more than a reflection of the shift occurring within you. As many masters of many traditions have said, "As it is within, so it is without."

Basically, I am an ordinary person. I was not born with any special spiritual gifts, and in fact I have been aspiritual most of my life. I grew up in a divided home. My father was a World War II veteran and my mother was a German war bride. The divisions of war lived on long past the Allied victory in an invisible, but emotionally, tangible dread that lingered in my house. If I exhibited any clairvoyance at all, it was to know whether it was safe to make an appearance or best to hide in my room. My mother attended a Lutheran church with some regularity, but my father never attended with her. I was dropped off one Sunday at an Episcopal church for religious training. It was my father's denomination, even though he did not attend that church. For me as a child, religion was just a random set of beliefs and experiences with no overriding meaning or significance.

I continued in this way well into adulthood. I would occasionally attend church and observe the behavior of devout followers. What I saw amounted to little more than a set of habits—going to church on Sundays, following preconceived rituals, and saying a prayer now and again. All of this offered nothing relevant to my daily life and did nothing to sooth the emptiness I felt in my heart.

Then all of that suddenly changed. For a brief moment the veil was pulled back, and I was able to glimpse that there was more—much more—to this existence than I had ever imagined. I will reveal more details to you as you read on about what happened in a graveyard for deceased nuns named Mary. The external events include a statue of the Virgin Mary and a bluebird. While these details have symbolic meaning, the most miraculous event happened within my heart. I had been opened and knew without any doubt that God's love was undeniably real, more real than anything I've experienced in this world. This prompted me to give up a highly successful corporate sales career to follow a new avocation in life, the results of which I will share with you in these pages.

I have discovered that what we call "ordinary" is actually full of extraordinary potential. Simple things we do all the time, like sitting down to have coffee with a friend, have infinite possibility of miraculous happenings. I see these miracles every day, so many that only a fraction of them can be included in this book. And I know that what I have experienced can be experienced by anyone. I have written this book because I believe that you do not need to wait for some divine intervention like I had in the cemetery. Divinity is already there in your life, waiting for you to embrace it!

The acronym S.A.I.N.T. summarizes the mindset needed to open completely to the experience of the Holy Spirit and to become a conduit of God's love in every moment of your life. S.A.I.N.T. consists of five simple principles that, when used conscientiously and consistently, will help you to realize God continuously. We will examine each element in detail in this book. To summarize:

S—Surrender—Know that God's plan is preeminent to the will of man, and relinquish your need to control events from the human perspective. "Let go and let God," as the saying goes.

A—Accept—Understand that all is in divine order and drop all emotional resistance or egotistic attachment to preconceived results.

I—Invite—Allow the presence of the Holy Spirit in whatever way it may manifest itself in this particular situation. Actively ask for Divine Presence through internal prayer, without demanding or begging.

N—Now—Keep your mind completely focused in the present moment. Drop any need to judge or analyze what is happening.

T—Trust—Have faith that all is unfolding as God intends. Know without a doubt that this is a sacred moment and embrace the sanctity of life itself.

I am asking you, through the process of S.A.I.N.T., to consider a different kind of knowing. Usually we learn about God by reading the Bible, attending church, and /or contemplating points of theology. As you know, our ways of defining God have led to great division and violence in the world. This is not a surprise, since it is not really possible to fit God into the cramped box of the human vocabulary. Trying to understand God through dogma, theology, and sacred texts is like trying to understand a watermelon through someone else's description of it.

S.A.I.N.T. allows you to know God in such a way that He becomes an integral part of your being, a divinity that follows you into every moment of your day. To understand a watermelon, you have to pick it up in your hands and take a big juicy bite. I am asking you to do the same thing in your relationship with God. Stop standing on the sidelines of spiritual experience. Be a saint now and experience the reality that God is.

Chapter One

OPENING UP

All human births are traumatic. Our memories of birth are shrouded from conscious memory, but it is not hard to imagine what it must have been like. For nine months you were warm and safe within the womb, all of your first sensations blunted by this enclosed, protected environment. You had no perception of the difference between your mother's body and your own. You simply existed without any individualized sense of self.

In a flash all of that changed. The womb that once protected you now sought to expel you, and you were pushed out into the cold outside world. You were born into a world that was very different from the simple state of being you had known. From that moment forward you began to learn about the nature of separation, realizing slowly, but surely, that you were now an individual entity unto yourself. The lesson of the separated human condition starts with our exit from our mother's body and continues as we are weaned, take our first independent steps, go off to school, until we grow up to live on our own.

Such is the case for all newborn babies coming into this human world. I was born into a world torn apart by war, perhaps the ultimate expression of separation between people. I was born in Germany at the end of World War II, the product of the union of enemies—a German mother and an American GI father. At that time much of Germany had been reduced to piles of rubble, and the Americans were no longer there to fight, but rather to assist in the reconstruction of post-war Germany. I can imagine that my parents came together because their main obsession of their young lives, the War, was over and both needed someone or something to turn their attentions. Theirs was a forbidden union, as relationships between US soldiers and Germans were forbidden as "fraternization with the enemy" until almost a year after my birth.

There are many romantic Hollywood tales of lonely American GIs bringing home a beautiful German *fraulein* to live happily ever after. Perhaps this was true for many of these couples brought together in the deconstructed landscape of the War's aftermath, but "happily ever after" was not to be for my parents. Love left the union as quickly as it had come, and the two were left bonded only by the legal demands of matrimony, parenthood, and little else.

Both of my parents had been married before, and both already had children. My mother had been widowed a couple of years earlier when her German husband was lost in the war. When she became pregnant with me early in their relationship, my father decided to divorce his American wife to create a new life with my mother. Only recently relieved from the horrors of war, my father found himself burdened with two small children and a new wife whom he did not really know. After returning to America and marrying her, a third child, another girl, would soon be added to the ranks. We became a fragmented family formed from opposing cultures and broken dreams.

It would not take long before my father would realize that he was not the love of my mother's life. Her true love had been ripped away from her, and my father was a second-rate substitute chosen by a woman in need. Many years later they would finally relent and divorce, but not before I was almost grown. In the meantime they would carry on their continuation of the war. It was not a war fought with guns and bombs, but the skirmishes were just as violent. Although we may have appeared as a normal American family on the outside, our household was one of constant verbal, physical, and emotional warfare.

I was the scapegoat for the brunt of my father's frustrations. After all, I was the one who landed him in this domestic jail. If it had not been for my conception, perhaps my parents' relationship would have been nothing more than a fleeting affair. On top of that, I was the middle child between two sisters from different fathers. I soon learned to read the energy of the household to judge when it was time to lay low or make an appearance.

Thus I learned from a young age to believe in the illusion of human separation from God. I had no understanding that God was real, and if He was, I assumed He was something far away from me. Still, there was always a glimmer of curiosity in the back of my mind, a thought that there might be something else that I couldn't quite perceive.

The division between my parents included spiritual life as well. I never once saw my parents attend church together, so there was little spiritual direction for us kids. My mother provided some sense of spiritual direction to us, but the circumstances made it difficult to cultivate. I would, on occasion, attend a Lutheran church with her, but it was so rare that the purpose and meaning of it remained a mystery to me. It was little more than a group of people in stiff shirts and Sunday hats acting a little more strangely than usual. My mother did the best she could to instill some sense of goodness in me but the strife of the marriage was too much to overcome. All of us struggled for something better than what we had. But what that might be was unclear.

One Sunday I was dropped off at an Episcopal church. Apparently this place was determined to be the best place for my spiritual education. I was simply delivered like a bag of laundry to the cleaners, presumably to ensure the fate of my immortal soul and my parents' obligation toward it. Neither of my parents had any affiliation there, and I was confined to the church basement, where, with other children, I listened to the ramblings of an older woman who told us how wonderful the world was and that she was so blessed to have such loving relatives. I completed my lessons like a good boy, was confirmed by the church, and that was that.

Those confirmation classes would be the last of my spiritual education for the next forty years. Christ walked for forty days in the desert, and you might say that I walked for forty years in my own kind of desert. I knew spiritual people here and there, but they remained plastic to me. I admired them on some level, but somehow nothing about that part of them seemed entirely real to me. The sense of separation I experienced as a boy became habitual, as perhaps it does for many people. Yet, an underlying spiritual ache persisted. I ignored the feeling, as one might learn to ignore a persistent case of bursitis.

All of this would suddenly and irrevocably change one summer's day in Wisconsin.

In the late 1990's I was living in a suburban neighborhood in southern Wisconsin while working for a telecommunications company. My wife and I shared a modest home in countryside of lush green fields and gently rolling hills. Several times a week I would go for a jog, following a path which led past an obscure and mysterious hill. A narrow paved road ran up this hill and I felt strangely drawn to it. Yet, at the same time, I felt pushed away. I wanted to run up the hill, but I was afraid to find out that I didn't have enough manly vitality left to pull myself up this hill. I felt safer to stay on my simple looping track.

One August day, the longing overcame me, and I made the turn up the hill. The one lane road leading up the hill steadily increased its grade as I made my way upward. I immediately began to feel the extra burn in my legs. "Oh no, you don't!" I silently told the hill as I summoned my determination to conquer the task before me. I focused on the rhythm of my stride to pound away any lack of confidence. The hill rewarded my determination with beautiful shade trees lining both sides of the asphalt road.

As I made my way up this hill, the trees became larger, their strong branches reaching out as if to touch the one opposite. Soon, they formed a complete canopy above me as I ran. The green leaves glowed like stained glass in an ancient cathedral, illuminated by the bright sun from behind. Occasionally shafts of lights penetrated the leafy mosaic to throw round spots of light on the road before me. Although my body was getting tired, I had the odd sense of my spirit lifting. Perhaps inspired by the sacred beauty before me, I thought momentarily of my church confirmation, something I had not thought of in years. My mind continued to vacillate from one topic to the next—one moment pondering my fitness to complete the physical challenge of the run, the next absorbed in some long forgotten memory.

I continued to slog up the hill, my body reaching exhaustion. I was determined not to stop, determined to prove that I still had what it took, determined to prove that middle age had not gotten the best of me. It was a grueling upward climb and each stride burned deeply into the muscles of my thighs and calves. At last I reached the top of the hill and entered a clearing beyond the trees. As I slowly came to a stop, I bent over, bracing against my knees. My breath blew like a locomotive and my heart pounded rapidly. I felt both exhilarated and exhausted by my achievement. "I still have it," I boasted to myself proudly. For that moment I was "King of the Hill," and I flung my arms over my head, waving them triumphantly to my audience of the trees that surrounded me. From this vantage point, I was offered a stunning vista of Wisconsin dairy lands. Puffy white clouds were floating above me in the azure sky, and I felt I was tall enough to touch them. Exhilarated by pride, my mind filled with thoughts of glory.

Suddenly, my internal cacophony of self-congratulation was silenced. My eyes were drawn to a lone statue, about six feet tall, standing in the nearby clearing. Curious, I walked toward it. It was the image of the Virgin Mary carved in white marble, standing perfectly straight with her head slightly bowed and her eyes opened but downcast toward the earth. Her palms were together with fingertips pointing to the sky, in a position of eternal prayer and devotion. She was clothed in a simple robe with a hooded shawl draped over her head. The shawl's edges were decorated with an ornate floral pattern. A long rosary was draped over her right hand, a tassel hung on a long rope from her neck, and a six-pointed star was displayed on her robe, just beneath her folded hands.

There she stood before me, a perfect image of serenity and devotion. I was instantly stunned and humbled by her appearance. Somehow, she encompassed the visual representation of many opposites at once—the hardness of the stone and the softness of her graceful femininity; the oldness of the marble's weathered surface and the youthfulness of her unwrinkled face; the intricate designs on her robe contrasting the simplicity of her unassuming pose.

I looked beyond her and saw row after row of marble grave markers planted low in a field of grass. Suddenly, I realized I was in a cemetery. I had run up this hill to prove my aliveness, only to come face to face with death. I had never been a praying man, yet in this instant I felt the urge to say a prayer for each of these departed souls.

The weariness of my body overtook me as I stood before the Blessed Virgin. I felt compelled to lie down on the grass in front of her. Her eyes were blank, yet I could not help being transfixed by them. As I lay there looking at this serene statue of Mother Mary, I thought of the service she was called to render. I imagined the scene of the Annunciation, the angel Gabriel informing Mary of Christ's birth through her. What must it have been like to be told by an angel that you would soon give birth to a child while still a virgin? In that day and age, it would have been a burden beyond compare. How could anyone give themselves to God with such unflinching devotion? It seemed impossible. Subconsciously, I knew that my soul had been called. I began to speak to Mary as though she were a living being.

"Mary, do you know that I don't attend church or even read the Bible? Certainly it is too late for me. There are others who worship you regularly. Certainly you mean to call them, not me." I felt like those words were being churned up from somewhere deep inside of me.

"I never really understood religion," I continued. "I was turned off by what I saw in church. Forgive me for saying these things. I am being honest. I don't mean to judge anyone's faith as false, but I have a mind that needs evidence. If what you are is true . . . and Jesus is who He says He is . . . can't you find some way to show me so that I can believe? Or is it too late for me?"

At that moment, I felt a chill run through my body—perhaps my body was cooling off after my run. Perhaps something more. I looked at Mary's eyes and implored of her, "I'm asking you for a sign, Mary! Nobody's here but us and the trees, and at this moment, for some reason I don't understand, I believe you can hear me. Is there anything you can show me, something to help me understand why I am feeling this way?" I looked up toward the heavens and asked, "Why don't you come out of the sky and show me something? I need an experience that will erase all doubt."

I felt relieved, my soul suddenly unburdened. I continued to lie there, gazing into Mary's eyes. My mother's favorite Bible verse came to mind, one that reflected her belief that prayer was the pathway to hope and understanding in this world. The verse (Matthew 7:7) reads: "Ask and it shall be given to you. Knock and it shall be opened to you." Those words echoed through my mind and heart in that moment of longing. I said to Mother Mary, "I know I'm asking the impossible. I know I'm not worthy of such grace, but if only you can show me proof of God's existence, I promise to follow Him the rest of my days and to honor you in all my thoughts and deeds."

I waited for the skies to open and reveal the heavenly host, but nothing happened. No voice of God from on high. No prophecy written in the sky. Just silence. I was glad that I asked, but who was I to expect anything? After a few minutes, I stood up and looked around. There were no teardrops of blood flowing from Mary's eyes. Nothing miraculous had happened.

I looked again at the grave markers and remembered my urge to offer a simple prayer to each of the people buried in the cemetery. I would keep my commitment, even if it seemed that my request for a sign, for "proof," had not been granted. Making my way toward the rows, I stepped over a few pine cones and piles of leaves that had gathered on the grass. Momentarily, a bird's feather caught my eye. It was small and gray with a vibrant blue hue on the edges and tip. I thought little of it and moved on.

As I neared the first row, I saw a bluebird sitting undisturbed by one of the markers. His head, wings, and tail were bright azure blue, his chest painted with a rusty red and pure white. I looked at the bluebird, and he looked at me. I then glanced down at the first gravestone, which read, "Sister Mary, 1847." "This is odd," I thought, surprised to see the name Mary after having been so intently focused on the statue. I realized this individual must have been a Catholic nun. I called her full name out loud before praying, "Sister Mary, thank you for your devout life of service to others, and may you forever rest in peace."

I then stepped to my right and was surprised to find that this marker also read "Sister Mary." "What kind of cemetery is this?" I wondered. The third stone was also inscribed with the name "Sister Mary," and then the next, and the next.

Making my way along the gravestones, I came closer and closer to the bluebird, still sitting on the marker. When I was within three feet of him, he flew away and landed a little further up the second row. I continued with my prayers, saying each sister's name, Mary, and asking God to bless and comfort her soul. All the while, I pondered the lives of service and devotion that these women led. I felt shallow and embarrassed among these holy servants. My life seemed small in comparison, and I felt the desire for devotion deepen within me.

Yet, I still desired some sign, some way of moving beyond my doubts. "Why am I here among these saintly people, standing on sacred ground?" I pondered. Still carrying my cut-off t-shirt and plastic bottle of Hawaiian Punch, I slowly made my way up the next row. I once again drew nearer to the bluebird, now nestled by another gravestone. "This is odd," I thought. "He isn't frightened of me." I dropped my t-shirt next to him; he sat undisturbed. I moved on. At gravestone after gravestone, I called the name, "Sister Mary" again and again. Fifty times, then one hundred, and finally more than two hundred times, I prayed for a "Sister Mary."

After forty-five minutes I had completed my prayers and went to retrieve my t-shirt. As I walked from the far corner grave back to the second row, I wondered if the bird was still there. He was. He sat in the grass as if he were waiting for me. He remained unafraid.

I was a giant compared to this small creature, but that was of no concern to him. I wondered if he was sick, but he appeared healthy. After waiting a moment, I decided to sit on an adjacent stone within two feet of this bluebird. The fluffy white feathers of his chest were pressed against my shirt lying crumpled on the ground. We sat silently for a moment, looking at each other.

Then I did what anyone would do. I talked to him. "What are you doing here?" I asked. "Why aren't you flying away? Don't you know that I'm human? You're supposed to be afraid of me!"

The bluebird stared at me as though I was the one that would fly away at any moment. Indeed, I felt unsettled. I picked up my Hawaiian Punch bottle and gulped down the last mouthful. A few drops remained, so I decided to offer some to my new little friend. I poured the drops into my flip-top lid and extended my arm.

To my surprise, the bird lowered its beak to the lid, lifted his head, and swallowed the red punch. I was amazed. He acted like I was an old friend. I sat in stunned disbelief. Something was shifting inside of me. The unbelievable had become believable; the unreal had become real.

After thirty minutes, I told my friend that I had to go home. I reached for my gray shirt. Surprisingly, the bluebird hopped onto it. He was in my hand as I stood up; his face was only inches from my own. "This is absolutely bizarre," I thought as I looked at the bird in disbelief. The bird was perfectly calm. I began to wonder if it was real or if I was losing my mind. I wrapped my shirt over his back as he nestled in my palm.

In my mind, I relived my run up the hill. It was a flash of memories—the glowing green leaves, my memories of confirmation, my boyhood pain, the burning in my muscles as I pounded my way up the hill, the exhilaration of accomplishment. I remembered that during my run, the number forty kept coming to me—the forty years I had been absent from church. I also remembered babbling to myself, speaking in a kind of tongues. One moment I felt like I was in Heaven, the next I was confessing to Mother Mary, and the next praying over nuns. This was certainly not the scenario I had expected when I set out on my jog that morning.

Then my eureka moment came! "There's a pattern. I get it!" I thought excitedly. I had asked

Mother Mary for a sign, something I could really believe in. I asked for a sign from the sky, and this bird came from the sky. "Oh, my God!" I thought. "This is a miracle!"

I rushed back to the statue of Mary and I lifted my hands up to her, still cradling the bluebird. My eyes filled with tears and a lump came to my throat. Choking on my words, I cried out, "This is my sign! No man made this possible. I believe you heard me!" The bluebird rose up, stretched out his wings, fluffed up his feathers, and then settled back in my hand. Somehow this motion communicated approval. I felt he understood what I was saying. I stood motionless. There was thundering silence as before. I looked at the feathered creature in my hand as tears of joy streamed down my face.

I turned and saw a house nearby. I walked toward it, still clutching this little bluebird. The house was just fifty yards from me at the other end of the clearing. I stepped onto the porch and knocked on the door. A man about my age answered. He was startled to see a half-naked stranger on his porch holding a bird. He looked at me curiously. Caught up in the moment, it didn't occur to me how strange I must have looked.

The man leaned forward to look closer at the bird. "It's a bluebird," he said, looking puzzled.

"Yes, it is," I replied. "I found him over there." I motioned my head toward the cemetery. Then I turned and moved my hands closer to the stranger.

"Interesting," he said, studying the little creature. The bluebird remained still, taking attention away from me. This man seemed to know something I didn't. He paused, and then faced me. Something struck him about what I had said. He stared at me intently, rubbing his chin with his hand, then said, "Blue is the color of the Virgin Mary."

"I didn't know that," I replied. I really had no idea about that. Again, I was taken by surprise, and my sense of amazement deepened. "Can this all be real?" I wondered.

I asked the man if he had any crackers or bread for the bird. He went inside and returned with some bread crumbs. He dropped a few in my left hand, so I placed one of the crumbs in front of the bird. The bird hesitated for a moment as the stranger and I waited for a reaction. The bluebird twitched his neck, and quickly pecked at the crumb. The man smiled, sharing my moment of astonishment.

"If he drinks wine, I would say we have something here," the man joked, his eyes transfixed on the bird. One crumb was enough.

The feathered creature stirred restlessly. I pulled my shirt away from his soft body, knowing it was time to let go. The bluebird jumped from my hand and flew off into the woods. My friend was forever gone. Silently I said goodbye to my bluebird, saddened to see him fly away. The stranger, whom I later found out to be a minister, offered a few words, something about God looking after even the lowliest sparrow. At the time I didn't understand him.

I had seen many miracles that day, but the biggest of all had occurred inside of me. The boy born in the hell of war had been reborn as a servant of heaven.

I believe that what I experienced on that hilltop was an example of the kind of miracles that await us every day. There is an "invisible window" separating the mundane and the divine that can be opened by anyone at any time. I wrote this book to help you open that window, the window that provides a view beyond that of limited human self. I have come to realize that my experience with the bluebird was a gift of grace through a moment of instantaneous surrendering. At the top of the hill I was "King of the Hill," yet wound up the servant of God! I ran up the hill to prove to my middle-aged self that I was still alive, only to look the reality of death right in the face as I stood in the cemetery. In the moment of a runner's pride, I found absolute humility. The window was flung wide open for me, and it can be opened for you, too.

Chapter Two

OPENING THE WINDOW

W hat do you think of when you think of a saint? Do you think of some figure from the Bible or a modern-day saint like Mother Theresa? Any of them can serve as a model for you. The important thing to realize about all of them is that they were just ordinary human beings who found exceptional grace. There is no need to create a false separation between them and yourself. They simply committed themselves to their path with complete devotion. When you do that, miracles *will* happen.

Mother Theresa is a good example because she lived in the modern era. We know she was real because we have seen news footage of her work, and unless you are very young, you lived on this planet during the time she was alive. She is your contemporary. Yet, most people believe that her level of commitment is beyond them. Mother

Theresa is a common example of a saint mentioned in casual conversation. But why not be a Mother Theresa? Perhaps you cannot imagine yourself walking among the poor of Calcutta as she did. Yet this in itself is not a deficiency. No saint's path has ever been the same, and your calling will be unique to you, according to God's plan for you. Unless you are called to it, you do not need to go to Calcutta or any other place burdened by disease or poverty. In fact, our Western culture, beset by its own sort of spiritual poverty, may be greater than the physical poverty of third world countries. You can easily find your own Calcutta in your own backyard.

When looking at the lives of saints, we often make the mistake of thinking that their works are what make them special. Journalist Malcolm Muggeridge, in his book *Something Beautiful for God*, wrote about Mother Theresa and the impact she had on people. He wrote, "I was watching the faces of people—ordinary people listening to her. Every face, young and old, simple and sophisticated, was rapt with attention, hanging on her words—not because of the words themselves, which were quite ordinary, but because of her. Some quality came across over and above the words. A luminosity seemed to fill the hall, penetrating every heart and mind." [1]

---

[1] Muggeridge, Malcolm. *Something Beautiful for God*. New York: Harper, 1986.

It was her presence among the people, her being, that really made the difference. She once said, "Not all of us can do great things. But we can do small things with great love." All Mother Theresa ever did was meet people, person to person, with great love, something they hungered for far more than bread. Love of this kind is a state of being, not an expression or something you do for someone. It is not dependent on a person being "loveable" in the ordinary sense, nor does it require anything in return.

The S.A.I.N.T. method is meant to help you cultivate this same state of being within yourself— not just for a moment of transcendence, but as a habitual part of life. In this state of being you will be able to open what I call the "invisible window," a portal connecting this limited physical world to the infinite spiritual dimension. It only requires the determination to shift your mindset away from self-service toward the service of others.

When you open this "window," the sense of separation between yourself and God will disappear. Likewise, any sense of separation between you and the people you interact with will disappear. Just as air flows freely inside and outside a window once you have opened it in your home, so too will the energy of your life and the world around you begin to flow. This is not about religion as we normally experience it, and it does not require any theological knowledge. Rather, it is about peering between the layers of existence into the realm of absolute divinity, beyond the three-dimensional world of limitations.

For me, opening the "invisible window" begins each day with a simple prayer. I pray, "God, please put in front of me this day the people You choose for me to meet and the circumstances I should embrace that I may serve You." Automatically, this prepares my mind to view everything and everyone I encounter in my day through the lens of divinity. I have seen countless wonders arise in my life as a result. Recognize God in the person before you and the possibilities for a spiritual connection will emerge. Here is one example of what can happen between people when the "window" is open.

One Sunday morning, I was visiting with friends at a local church after the service. We stood outside with our coffees in hand, exchanging light conversation about our lives and the ways of the world. By late morning the group disbanded, and we headed in our own directions. I lingered for a while, talking to the remaining few until it was time to go.

As I slowly made my way to my car I noticed a man walking toward me from the far end of the parking lot. He appeared to be about fifty, a rather large man, just over six feet tall and heavyset. He called, "Good morning!" He walked closer offering a broad friendly smile. "My name is David," he said, introducing himself.

"Hello," I answered, not sure of his intention. "I'm Charles. You don't look familiar. Are you visiting?"

"Yes," he bellowed in a deep tone as he extended his thick arm for a handshake. "I've come up from Phoenix for the weekend. It sure is beautiful here in Sedona compared to that sweatbox."

David stood directly in front of me in the empty parking lot. He seemed like a gentle giant to me. I chuckled at his description of Phoenix. "It's a sweatbox all right, maybe a 110 degrees today," I agreed.

It occurred to me that this was a person God had sent to me in answer to my morning prayer. This recognition opened the door for the Holy Spirit to guide me. Instantly, a subliminal pathway connected our souls. I was given the opportunity to meet David and recognize God within him.

"So David," I asked directly, "What brings you to this church parking lot today?"

"I'm staying over there," he replied, pointing toward a neighboring motel. "I just started walking after breakfast and ended up here."

"Are you with family?" I asked.

"No, I don't have any family that I am close to. My father died several years ago. My mother passed away last month and I have a stepsister who lives in Dallas. I'm pretty much alone."

"I'm sorry to hear about your mother, David."

David's easygoing demeanor suddenly changed as he deflected my condolences with an abrupt response.

"My mother and I were not close," he scoffed. "She married my father because of me being born, and they had a terrible relationship—lots of abuse and fighting. She blamed me for her misfortunes."

His reply startled me. Hearing that his parents married because of him being born and having parents, who fought, sounded a lot like my own experience.

I opted to redirect his thoughts by asking him about his stepsister. "Do you and your sister keep in touch?"

"Not if I can help it!" David snapped, even more repulsed. "My sister is a selfish woman. In fact, when my mother died, my sister didn't even mention me when she wrote her obituary. But I don't care. That's all behind me now."

David expressed coldness toward his family. Although he was an adult, he projected the demeanor of a hurt child. His suppressed feelings blew at me, like an open steam valve releasing pressure. I felt David was reaching out to me. I wanted to help him get past his feelings of family rejection and resentment. I offered him what I felt he needed—love and compassion.

David's flare-up subsided and he became more subdued. He seemed self-conscious about what he had revealed to me, perhaps thinking he said more than he should have.

"I'm sorry to hear that you've been so rejected, David, but I love you," I said hoping to offer some comfort.

Unexpectedly David shook, like he had been zapped by an electric charge. He suddenly lunged at me and kissed me on the cheek. I was overwhelmed by his emotional outburst. He lowered his head to my shoulder and wept loudly, tears flowing freely. He leaned his full weight against me, heaving and trembling. I didn't know what to think as I tried to prop him up. All I could do was anchor into my belief that God wanted me to help this man.

"It's okay, David. This is why we were to meet," I said compassionately. "When I told you I loved you, I was expressing a higher love to you—my ability to see God in you. Sometimes humans fail us but God never does. Try to forgive your family. Forgiveness will allow you to move on with your life."

David stepped back and wiped his eyes. "Thank you," he said in a quiet tone. "I don't know what came over me. When you said, 'I love you,' it caught me by surprise. It triggered something inside of me."

"I suppose it was time for you to have those feelings out," I replied. "Let me explain what prompted me to say that to you. In my morning prayer, I ask God to put in front of me the one He chooses for me to meet each day, and right now this person is you. You are God's choice for me to meet. That's why I said I love you."

David returned a big smile. "Yeah, maybe that's why I drifted over this way. I felt like I was being led here for a reason. What you said makes sense. I think we were supposed to meet here. Are you the minister of this church?" he asked.

"I have a sort of ministry, but it's not with this church," I answered him. "I've had these experiences for many years. I just go about my days normally, but when God chooses for me to meet someone, things happen. You and I have met in the middle of an empty parking lot—I believe by God's grace."

"But how do know when these things are going to happen for you?" David asked.

"I don't know. I turn each day over to God. The rest unfolds according to His plan. He chose for you and me to meet for a reason, for you to let go of family rejection and feel God's love for you. To rely on human love can be disappointing. God gives us all the love we need."

Soon David and I departed. I headed for home, and he walked back to the motel. The miracle of healing, to whatever degree God had granted it to David that day, had been accomplished.

Transformation of this type happens not through *doing*, but through *allowing*. When addressing the deepest needs of those around you, it is only through grace that personal defenses can come down and real healing can occur. The good news is that this grace is provided in droves through the Holy Spirit. The Holy Spirit is always available, if you are willing to open to Him.

You must be determined, however, to get your ego-self out of the way. This begins with the realization that you are not your body. Your true, immortal essence is spiritual, not physical in nature. The foundation of S.A.I.N.T. is love and compassion, and this requires love of self and the acknowledgement of your own spirit nature. This, of course, does not mean becoming puffed up with pride. Nor does it mean presenting yourself as spiritually "special." In fact, recognition of your spirit nature, if genuine, will generate both love of self, as well as deep, abiding humility. True confidence emerges from this recognition, as well as the ability to desire true love and goodwill for others.

Once you have recognized your own spirit, you will be able to do the same for the people who come before you. Regardless of their current condition, God dwells within them, just as He does within you. Some people, to the ordinary eye, may appear to be the lowest of the low—addicted, angry, weak, pathetic, parasitic, victimized, resentful, perverted, delusional, greedy . . . you name it. However, the only way you can touch any of them at the deepest level of their hearts is to see beyond that portrayal as the false façade it is. Any human being that is before you, whoever he or she is, has a divine spark and is equally deserving of love.

Opening up to the Holy Spirit allows transformation of your inner energy. Because you, too, are part of Spirit, the Holy Spirit is not a separate entity from you, even though it may feel as though that is the case. By allowing the Holy Spirit to enter through a relationship, you become *holy* in the truest sense of the word. The word "holy" comes from a Germanic word meaning "wholeness," so when you are in a "holy" state you are one with your true self, your divine nature. All divisions within yourself and between people are transcended in this state. Often people experience this state of being for fleeting moments—for example, when observing great natural beauty or when feeling great joy upon the birth of a child— however, it need not be a rare or overly abstract experience. It can be a continual state of being, which is the intended outcome of the S.A.I.N.T. practice.

But how can we know when the "invisible window" is really open? You will know when it happens because the experience will become embedded within you. In that moment, it will seem like time has stopped. Life ordinarily passes us by like frames in a movie reel as it is projected onto the screen before us. The images fly by, moment after moment, so we do not register the details of each individual frame. As a result, we forget to see each other and the moments of our lives are instead engrossed in the illusion. Yet, we can examine each frame if we choose to take the time to do so, just like we can take a scene from a movie and turn it into a snapshot.

Most of us remember, for example, certain famous scenes from the movie *Gone with the Wind* because they have been turned into iconic images in our minds. The moments of your life can be internalized in a similar way. When you open yourself to the Holy Spirit, you are choosing to step for a moment beyond the confines of time and space. In our physical lives we live in real time, but spiritually we need to slow down and examine each frame. Each frame in turn becomes eternal and infinite.

You have probably already experienced this during important moments, when time slowed down and a memory was etched forever into your brain. A common example is the experience of love at first sight. I, for instance, can remember perfectly the exact moment in time when I first met my wife. Many years would pass before we would enter into an actual relationship, yet the transcendent part of our relationship was already in place, even if the physical reality was not yet manifest.

I can remember that moment as if it happened one minute ago, and I can recall the details of the scenario like it was a photograph in my mind. My future wife was working as a hostess in a college dining hall. I saw her in the distance and was captured by something inside of me that knew without knowing in my conscious mind. That image of her all those years ago is still etched in my mind's eye with perfect clarity. I can see her as though she is standing before me, just by recalling the memory. There she stands—just over five feet tall, beautiful long blond hair, a glowing angel before me! The instant connection was like a camera's flash, and is imbedded within my soul.

At the time I had no understanding of the "invisible window," but it was real nonetheless. It was a random experience of connection at the time. I have now come to realize that such experiences are available to us at any time. Now, when I encounter a person in my life, I imagine a frame drawn around them, like the frame around a window. By doing so I make a clear decision to see them, not as their imperfect human self, but through the lens of divinity. Hence I am able to experience them in their true essence. Everything about them and the encounter is impressed onto my mind, and we become one for that moment.

Often I am able to recall minute details of an encounter much later, and people ask me if I have a photographic memory. Actually, I have no particular talent for memory; rather, I am wholly and completely present to the other person in that moment. After that, my mind simply catalogs the captured image of the "window" for future reference. I absorb this flash of true connection through the "invisible window." It provides the opportunity to see a lot of things in a pure way.

What I have described here, (what I call the opening of the "invisible window"), is the core of the practice I am recommending. S.A.I.N.T. is a way of getting ready to make the "invisible window" habitually present in your life. Anyone can open the "invisible window," but it does require a purification of sorts. You will learn how to cast aside aspects of yourself that limits your ability to love. Through S.A.I.N.T., you will be able to stand in the eye of the storm and be a beacon to all around you, regardless of the world's insanity or the circumstances of your own life. S.A.I.N.T., in essence, facilitates a cleaning of the will and intellect and allows you to let go of all fears, desires, and selfish motives. And when you have let go of those things, you will find that you have gained everything.

Chapter Three

THE FIVE PRINCIPLES OF S.A.I.N.T.

S tanding before the statue of Mother Mary at the graveyard, I doubted myself because I looked back on my past and made the mistake of thinking that was the sum total of who I am. If you feel unworthy, shift your perspective away from your earthly self toward your heavenly self. There is nothing you have done in the past that can disqualify you from sainthood *now*, because nothing you have done can detract from your soul or sully it in any way.

Faith is the only prerequisite to the practice of S.A.I.N.T., especially faith in yourself and your own soul. You must believe in the reality of your own divine life and in the divinity of all humankind because you are, as the book of Genesis states, "created in the image of God." People often say everyone is a "child of God," but how often do we live as though this is true? S.A.I.N.T. helps you to live that reality by getting past the limitations of the human self.

There is a striking scene from the movie *Avatar* that illustrates the nature of spirit-centered interaction between people. In the scene, the male protagonist, a human, looks deeply into the eyes of the female Na'vi character, and says with great sincerity, "I see you." She returns the same statement to him: "I see you." It is clear that these two characters are seeing each other beyond the limits of their physical selves. They feel love for each other that goes beyond even romantic love. They are characters from two completely different planets. They have vastly different bodies, and they don't even breathe the same air. Yet, through the love that they feel, they are able to see the other's true self, the soul inhabiting the body.

This scene is memorable because it represents the highest kind of love, something we are all craving. People need to be seen for who they truly are, to have their soul recognized, rather than being identified as the imperfect self of body and personality. Most of the unhappiness in today's world is rooted in the tendency to do the opposite, looking only at the person's outer condition. This habit is especially damaging when we focus only on negative traits of another person. It is equally a mistake to identify a person's value with their positive attributes. Ultimately, we are all far more than the sum total of our habits, errors, personality, status, talents, etc. Beyond all these masks lies our real identity, a soul far more vast than anything of this world. If you fully recognize the divine nature of others around you, they will recognize their own, and real healing can begin.

S.A.I.N.T. is the process of being "born again," of becoming reacquainted with one's "higher self." We are born with this spirit essence; however in many people it is practically dead. Of course, your soul never actually dies, but it can seem that way when we misappropriate our mortal human self as our main identity. We falsely believe that we are a small being separated from God, floating alone on a tiny planet in a vast universe. As a result, we cling to degraded images of ourselves made up of social status, job titles, and other human concerns. To be stuck in such a perception is to feel alone in the most profound way and this is at the root of loneliness that so many feel in today's world.

But we are not alone. S.A.I.N.T. offers a path back to God, a return to a non-separation from God. It is a rebirth into the dimension of the Holy Spirit.

John 3:3 reads, "Verily, verily, I say unto thee, except a man be born again, he cannot see the kingdom of God." Being "born again" is the willingness to drop the pretenses of human life and the defenses of the human ego. It is like a rebirth because you must return to your essential nature, like a newborn baby who has yet to adopt the preconceptions and illusions of the world. This is the process of death-to-self that any spiritual path requires. And you may need to "die" to your old self and be "born again" many times in your process of growth.

This cycle of death and rebirth is demonstrated through Christ's death and resurrection. He was born into earthly form precisely to demonstrate the cycle of death and rebirth that we must all embody in our lives. It is symbolically appropriate that I found myself in a graveyard when it was time to be born again, and likewise your old egoistic self must die in the process of becoming a saint. The New Testament of the Bible compares the process of death and rebirth to a seed dropping to the ground. John (12:24-26 KJV) reads:

> Verily, verily, I say unto you, except a corn of wheat fall into the ground and die, it abideth alone: but if it die, it bringeth forth much fruit. He that loveth his life shall lose it; and he that hateth his life in this world shall keep it unto life eternal. If any man serve me, let him follow me; and where I am, there shall also my servant be: if any man serve me, him will my Father honor.

This is an appropriate analogy for those following the S.A.I.N.T. model since you will indeed be planting seeds of hope in the hearts of the people you meet as you begin to embody S.A.I.N.T. principles. At the same time, you will find yourself growing as the seed of your own soul develops in fertile soil. Like the seed that never drops into the soil to sprout new life, a soul that never feels its divine spark has wasted its potential.

S.A.I.N.T. will help you live your soul's potential, and you will in turn help others discover their own. Often, you may not know what the result of your practice is. In some people, the seed planted will grow into a beautiful flower; others might neglect to water that seed and it may not flourish. Regardless of the outcome, it is the purity of your intention that matters, because that fosters growth in *you*. God has a plan for all of us and each individual has the free will to accept or deny the call of his soul. In the final analysis, S.A.I.N.T. is not at all a path of sacrifice or self-denial because the benefits to you will be immense.

The acronym S.A.I.N.T. is meant to help you ingrain these essential principles into your mind so that they become an automatic part of your life. S.A.I.N.T. is only useful if your understanding of the principles goes beyond the intellectual "book learning" level to become part of who you are.

These principles are meant to be *lived*, not just studied.

The S.A.I.N.T. principles are repeated three times and that is intentional. The first step is simple memorization. Be familiar enough with the meaning to repeat it easily to yourself, especially when you are facing a difficult situation. After that, you can study the deeper implications of each of the principles: *surrender, accept, invite, now* and *trust*. Finally—and most importantly—you put S.A.I.N.T. into practice in your daily life. Circumstances may make this difficult on occasion, so use S.A.I.N.T. to bring your mind back into its proper focus. With time, they will become integrated into your subconscious mind and will become automatic.

Let's look at each of the five principles in a little more detail.

S—SURRENDER: True surrender can be summed up by the well-known line from the Lord's Prayer: "Thy will be done." It sounds simple, but surrendering is one of the most difficult principles for people to follow because most have the habit of trying to resist or control the world around them. This is the nature of the human ego, which continually tries to rearrange reality for its own benefit. "Surrender" means letting that part of you die so that you can turn any situation over to the Holy Spirit. Surrender to that which is, even if you don't like the way things are. Acknowledge the perfection of God's plan, even though your human eyes may see suffering, chaos, corruption, and all sorts of perceived imperfection. Through surrender the veil of worldly concern is lifted from your own holiness.

The S.A.I.N.T. method recommends two specific practices to facilitate surrender: First, during Morning Prayer, ask for God to put in front of you the people He intends for you to meet. Through this request you are acknowledging that every person you encounter is there by divine appointment. Make no attempt to chase after someone or to force yourself or your ideals upon a person. If you have truly surrendered, there is no reason to be caught up by what you think "should" be happening.

Second, ask that God present you with the circumstances that you are to embrace, without any judgment of "good," "bad," "right," "wrong," etc. Embrace each circumstance with loving acceptance, even if it seems uncomfortable to you at first. If you are uncomfortable, know that God has guided you there for some reason particularly appropriate to your own and the other person's maturation process.

A—ACCEPT: Acceptance is closely related to surrender, but suggests a deeper acknowledgement of God's plan. Sometimes we surrender to God's will but do not accept it fully. Even after we stop trying to control a situation, we continue to resist it within ourselves. This sort of resistance may consciously and unconsciously block our ability to be a conduit of the Holy Spirit.

Inability to accept is rooted in the human tendency to judge that which we experience and perceive. Our human brains are geared toward dualities, dividing the world into opposites—good/bad, right/wrong, ugly/beautiful, worthy/unworthy, etc. The divine mind, however, exists beyond the three dimensional world. God knows the big picture of existence, and so do our souls. Thus, to stay in a state of non-acceptance is to bind your level of thinking to the earthly level. Let go of that, and your consciousness can rise to the level of heaven.

Acceptance, of course, does not mean embracing that which is harmful or immoral. Discernment is always necessary on our earthly path, but this does not mean we have to withhold love or compassion from anything. And if you feel the need to take proactive action to improve some condition in the world, by all means do so. The difference lies with you as you face negative situations with a positive heart.

You may face many difficult situations in life: a friend loses his job, a daughter severs a relationship, or a neighbor endures a home foreclosure, for example. These are all difficult, yet when they are accepted as being God's divine will, the perception shifts to one of greater possibilities. The difficulties of life become the impetus for growth, not a reason for despair. Change is a natural current of life, and if you accept this flow rather than push against it, you discover a hidden treasure within yourself as faith emerges.

I—INVITE: When you are in a state of surrender and acceptance, it is important to ask for intervention from a higher source, namely, the Holy Spirit. Otherwise, you will be directed only by your own energy, not God's. The Holy Spirit refers to the belief held in the Abrahamic religions. For the majority of Christians, the belief in the Holy Spirit implies the existence of three distinct holy persons being one eternal Triune God. The Holy Spirit acts as an agent of divine action or communication, the pure essence of God's attributes. The Holy Spirit, also called the "Comforter," fills you with calm and peace. In this state of grace, inspiration will flow through you. The Holy Spirit will provide whatever words of comfort or advice that you or the other person needs. If you get yourself out of the way and invite the Holy Spirit to be present, you never need worry about saying the right words and doing the right thing. In your state of openness you have invited the Holy Spirit to literally guide you.

Once you are infused with the Holy Spirit you will be able to express joy to others. Try not to over analyze the inspiration that comes; just embrace it, even if you have no idea of its deeper meaning. At times you may express this invitation to the person with you as the Holy Spirit uses you to convey His message to the other person. In this way, through open invitation for inspiration, you can become a light to others. The Holy Spirit flows through you and directs you to the awareness of now, where each experience becomes a framed image imbedded into your consciousness.

N—NOW: Spiritual teachers have often rightly pointed out that the only real time we have is the present moment. People tend to focus everywhere else but in the NOW. We dwell on hurts and mistakes of the past or become embroiled in plans for the future. The only way to effectively be in the present, that is to be present and awake to your surroundings, is to focus on the NOW. There is no reason to focus on the past or future because they can sabotage the present moment. Allow yourself to become utterly lost in the present—immersed, concentrated, and fascinated.

Being in the NOW will allow you to experience true aliveness. Because you have invited the presence of the Holy Spirit, you will realize the presence of God in all that surrounds you. All of your senses will fully merge, you will see the spring flowers blossom, smell their fragrance, and hear the buzzing of the honeybees. All of your being is here to experience God, and NOW is the moment to do so.

T—TRUST: Trust is both the end and the beginning of the S.A.I.N.T. process. Trust allows you to embrace all of the other steps and enables you to come back to them again when you are beginning to doubt. Doubt, hesitancy, procrastination and delay result in missing out. To trust is to step out of your temporal mind and expand your spirit to the possibilities of the supernatural. TRUST is like a lighthouse that guides us continually back to God, regardless of how stormy life becomes.

This kind of trust is the gift of your open heart, not of your activist mind. While the mind hopes to prove God exists, the heart *reveals* God to you. Trust relieves you of a mind-controlled will and guides your actions through spirit. Just as a foundation underneath a house gives it strength, TRUST is the bedrock upon which the whole system is built.

By committing to S.A.I.N.T., you are committing to a spiritual discipline. You should be commended for that, because most people simply adopt a dogma that is either intellectually appealing or culturally familiar to them. But S.A.I.N.T. has little use as a life philosophy unless it is actually applied. This is a way of living, not a theology.

Applying the principles of S.A.I.N.T. in your daily life, you become a true disciple, not of some guru, but a disciple of the principles themselves. To become a disciple is to commit to true learning of the principles, not just a shallow book-learning of conceptual information. S.A.I.N.T. is not a discipline as in "punishment," but rather a commitment to learn. The root word for both *discipline* and *disciple* is the Latin *discere,* meaning "to learn" or "grab hold of." S.A.I.N.T. is a simple way to learn the true meaning of spirit life and to grab hold of it within yourself.

Your journey will probably be a lot like that jog I took up the hill in Wisconsin. At first, you may not even be sure you want to go up the hill. That is understandable since you don't really know what you will encounter, and it will be arduous at times. In the end, however, it will be worth it.

As a saint, you have become a beacon to others. You are capable of this only because you have faith and have surrendered yourself to higher principles. You encourage others, comfort others, defend others, energize others, and motivate others. You have this ability because you are gifted with some special charisma, which is that you have allowed the Holy Spirit to flow through you. The Holy Spirit has provided these things to you, and you are simply passing them forward.

Ultimately, no one can tell you how your path will look because everyone's calling is unique. The duration of every journey is the same, a meeting with your highest self. These are a few things you can expect.

1. Expect to go places you have never been and do what you have never done before. This is a path that is meant to challenge your limitations as it gives you opportunities to overcome them.

2. Expect to give more than you have ever given. This does not mean you have to give up money or any kind of physical comfort. You must, however, be willing to give time and energy to others. But remember—to give is to receive.

3. Expect to shed your attachments and preconceptions. This path is about removing the veils of perception that prevent us from loving others fully. You cannot cling to your biases and expect that to happen.

4. Expect to love like you have never loved before. You will be called to love strangers, including ones who are unworthy in the eyes of most other people. You will also be asked to forgive those whom you have failed to forgive.

5. Expect to learn true meaning of faith. To be successful on this path, to trust in the Holy Spirit is imperative. You will discover that the Holy Spirit penetrates and binds

together all things. To trust in the Holy
Spirit is to trust in the goodness of life.

6. Expect to become reacquainted with your
   spirit self. Although helping others is part
   of this path, the true alchemy is happening
   within yourself as your ego self gives way
   to your true spirit self.

Chapter Four

SURRENDER

Having been born in Germany in the aftermath of World War II, it now occurs to me that we are all born into a world of war. Even if there is political peace among nations, humans are constantly in a state of spiritual armed resistance. We go to war not only against nations but also against ideologies, religions, denominations, political parties and other individuals, including our family members. We even go to war against ourselves, saying we should be something other than what we are.

God made the earth and said, "It is good." We look at His creation and say the opposite. We look around ourselves and want to change everything to suit our personal preferences and ideals, thus putting ourselves in a state of resistance against that which *is*. In essence, our egos go to war against the present reality of God's creation, which places us in a state of war against God Himself. This creates a great amount of unnecessary suffering, especially within us.

How then do we escape this internal war? How does one get rid of this constant upset and state of resistance? In the Germany I was born into, the war had ended because the German leaders finally realized that they could not recreate the world according to their own egoism. We think of them as something "evil" and far away from ourselves. In reality the Germany of World War II was just an outward, mass expression of the war most people wage upon the world around them every day. There is only one way to end the war within yourself, the same choice that ended World War II: You must *surrender*.

This book offers guidelines for living a more saintly life, but you will notice that there are few specific requirements which are meant to fit into any lifestyle. Following S.A.I.N.T. is a spiritual routine. The expression of this discipline is ultimately up to you. There is one simple practice that I do recommend—prayer of surrender.

Each morning I say the simple prayer, "God, please put in front of me this day the people You choose for me to meet and the circumstances I should embrace that I may serve You." You can use these words or adjust them to be comfortable for you, so long as the essential meaning remains. The important idea is not the words of the prayer itself, but the state of being it invokes within you. For me, when I pray this prayer to myself, a shift of consciousness occurs within me. Suddenly, all pretenses are dropped, and I am completely open to God's will becoming manifest within my life, without expectation or prejudgment about what that should look like.

This prayer is similar to the prayer that Christ taught His followers to use, commonly known as the Lord's Prayer. The core principle of this prayer is delivered in the lines, "Thy kingdom come, / Thy will be done, / on earth as it is in heaven." These lines suggest a complete surrendering to God's will for your life and for the world. Some people have a habit of praying for things that they personally want or need, but notice that the words, "my will be done" do not appear in the prayer. As the prayer suggests, heaven on earth cannot be accomplished until we relinquish our personal motives to God—to "let go and let God."

I have learned through this practice that the "bad" situations of life can be transformed into powerful moments when we drop our resistance. This is not to say that I wish difficult things upon myself, but I have seen how they can ultimately be of service to those involved.

I remember one time I was driving and suddenly had a flat tire. Like anyone might be, I was annoyed by the situation. I pulled into a motel parking lot to call for help and was told a tow truck would arrive as soon as it could. There was nothing more that I could do but wait. As I sat on the concrete curb, I remembered my morning prayer and settled back into a state of surrender.

As soon as I did, a woman, one of the motel guests, came over and began to talk to me. I immediately recognized her as God's choice for me to meet. She told me she and her mother were visiting Sedona from Canada. Our conversation quickly moved from idle chatter to heartfelt revelation. She had broken off a relationship with a man who was abusive and she was trying to regain her self-esteem. Although talking about this with her mother was helpful, she didn't want to disrupt their vacation time with her personal issues. I provided another release for her emotions, so this moment provided great relief to her. Time seemed to stand still for us as we talked to each other for an hour. She thanked me and returned with a lighter heart to her room. Then, as if on cue, the tow truck arrived to assist me with my tire. The perfection God's plan for this inconvenient annoyance was now absolutely clear to me.

Surrender is a process, and is something you will need to return to again and again. It is normal and natural to find yourself in resistance to certain conditions of life, but it is only through surrender of that resistance that we can move forward. Essentially, it is a process of unwinding attachments and preconceptions. As we grow up in this human life, we develop our self-centered identity with all its desires for comfort, recognition, protection, etc. We crave the things of this world, even if those things are in conflict with our higher selves. Yet God teaches us to be "In the world and not of it." The ego teaches us to live for the needs of the limited body, even while something inside tells us there is something more. Thus, surrender requires the deep knowing that the needs of the soul are greater than the needs of the body. In other words, you must be willing to put the will of heaven ahead of the will of the world.

Surrender is not always easy. It requires a shift—sometimes a radical shift—from self-centered living to selfless living. Jesus Christ, in His willingness to surrender His life for the sake of others, provided the ultimate example of surrender. You, too, will likely be asked to give up something, perhaps a lot of things. These things can range from the willingness to give up your sense of superiority to making major life adjustments. There may be just one thing you must surrender, but more likely there will be many more. You must devote yourself to your own growth to find out what those things are and retrain yourself to live in a new way.

Matthew 16:24-27 quotes Christ: "If anyone would come after Me, let him deny himself and take up his cross and follow Me. For whoever would save his life will lose it, but whoever loses his life for My sake will find it. For what will profit a man if he gains the whole world and forfeits his soul?" This is a call to action, not a call to passive worship.

The requirement to deny self and to "take up the cross" is often forgotten in our spiritual lives. When looking at the life of Christ, we too often take a passive view of His life. We worship Him and praise Him, but we do not emulate Him. He becomes a flat symbol of what we wish we were, but are not. A more dynamic view of Christ is as a model for human behavior. Why else would God become flesh, to become a man walking upon the earth, unless His life is meant to be an example to us. We are not meant to merely worship, but to live the life that Christ demonstrated to us. We are all called to the life of a saint.

The cemetery was a place where my "self" had to die. Just as Christ symbolically demonstrated this "death of the ego" through His death and resurrection, He went through his own process of surrender as He realized the task before Him. In the Garden of Gethsemane He prayed, "Not my will, but yours be done," all the while knowing that He was bound to die. His final moments of life upon the cross, He said, "Into Your hands I commend my Spirit." In surrendering our very lives into the hands of God, we become Christ-like in a very real sense.

There was a woman called the Peace Pilgrim who demonstrated Christ-like surrender. Born with the name Mildred Lisette Norman, she was the daughter of poor parents in New Jersey. She was an ordinary woman who lived a typical lifestyle, until one day she felt called to change the direction of her life to serve humanity in some way. From 1955 to 1981 she walked more than 25,000 miles, just talking to people about inner peace.

Peace Pilgrim states in her booklet, *Steps Toward Inner Peace*, "I felt a complete willingness, without any reservations, to give my life, to dedicate my life to service. After that, you can never go back to completely self-centered living." [2] The message she delivered was a simple one: overcome evil with good, hatred with love, and falsehood with truth. In the process of spreading her message, she crisscrossed the country seven times.

When Peace Pilgrim dedicated her life to service, she surrendered everything, including her physical comfort. When she started walking, she had no money—only the clothes on her back. She was determined to "walk until given shelter and fast until given food." The spirit within her called her to this mode of service, and she gave herself to it without reservation. She was prepared to face any kind of difficulty, even homelessness

---

[2] http://www.peacepilgrim.org

and hunger. In the end she inspired the best in others and they always gave her food and shelter.

The surrender you make must be genuine, from deep within yourself. Take the moments of your life one at a time and examine them. What attachments need to be shed? Slowly but surely, retrain yourself to make everyday decisions from the perspective of the soul, not the ego. Be kind and patient with yourself. Even Peace Pilgrim did not give up her old life all at once. She required a 15-year preparation time for her personal process of surrender.

Please do not think that you must come up with something dramatic or extreme to live your life as a saint. If you have a genuine calling to something unusual, you will know it, but this is not typical. People like Peace Pilgrim are the exception, not the rule. We need a few people like her to really catch our attention to get us to ask whether or not we are on our correct path. Ultimately, it is more important that people be willing to live the life of the saint in the context of a normal life. Only when we call upon our spirit essence in an everyday context will life really change. The Peace Pilgrims of the world are wonderful models, but clearly we don't need a million people walking back and forth across the country. However, we do need people who get up in the morning, go to work, take their kids to school, do the dishes, and all the rest—but have a determination to connect to their own divinity and that of others in every moment. In this way, you can be a true Peace Pilgrim in your own way.

This will require some process of surrendering, no matter who you are. No matter how mundane your calling may appear to be, surrendering is always an internal process. It's not about planning an itinerary for an exotic adventure. It is, however, about "letting go" of that which your soul no longer needs, that which no longer serves your higher self. Especially in the modern world, we make our minds and our lives overly complex by adopting a tangle of attachments. Only you can decide which ones must be surrendered.

On my personal path, I have made surrender a daily part of my practice. It started with the decision to jog up that hill, to choose a path unfamiliar to me, and it has continued in that way ever since. My physical mind is given to doubt and skepticism, but I have also always heard the call of my soul. In my case, this meant giving up my job and changing my life completely. My ego mind was always there to tell me to be sensible, but in the end I knew I had to let go. I knew I had to follow the voice of my heart, not the voice of my head.

I felt called to give my life in service to God, but I had no certification, no divinity degree, and no outer confirmation of qualification. So my head balked. I had responsibilities. I had worked my way up to the top of my corporate sales career. I was not the "religious type." I had a wife to think of. How could I be considering such a thing? Yet, the call kept coming, even in my dreams at night. Little by little, I surrendered myself to God, and I have never looked back.

I have seen the power of surrender in the people I interact with every day. Surrender, if genuine, has the power to transform external circumstances instantaneously and can give rise to remarkable synchronicities.

Once I visited a Catholic church during the funeral service of a person I didn't know. After the service the mourners filed out of the church toward the cemetery. I remained in the church and sat quietly as an expression of devotion and contemplation.

While I was there, I noticed a woman in her late thirties standing in an alcove before a portrait of Our Lady of Guadalupe—Mother Mary for the Americas. She stood there sobbing, tears flowing down her face. I could see that she was wracked with sadness. Eventually, I walked over to talk with her. "Did you know the person well? Is this why you are crying?" I asked.

"No," she said. "I'm not here for the funeral. It's something else entirely."

She was crying because of a relationship that had just ended, leaving her alone with two young children. At that moment, I felt inspired to tell her my thoughts of surrender.

"Just surrender your problems over to God," I told her as we walked to the back of the church.

When I said this, she suddenly stopped crying, and she looked surprised. "I just recorded a song yesterday, one I wrote myself!" she exclaimed. "May I sing it for you?"

"Of course," I answered, startled by her change in behavior. "What is your song about?"

She looked at me with wide eyes and answered . . . "Surrender." She sang the song for me, and her voice rang like an angel throughout the church. I could see in her eyes that she was truly hearing the words of her own song for the first time. When she finished, her demeanor was strikingly serene and peaceful. We talked for a few minutes, said a brief prayer, hugged each other and then departed.

One month later, I was visiting a different church on Sunday when I heard familiar words playing over the outdoor sound system. I looked inside the church and there was this same woman singing her song to the congregation. She looked happy and confident as she sang "Surrender." After the service we reconnected with a hug and looks of surprise and joy. We were soon joined by her handsome new beau and I witnessed the new life she had created. Her life had transformed completely in a very short time.

This woman's revelation about her own song is not unlike how we all experience our spiritual lives. She had actually written these lyrics but had failed to apply them in her own life. Like her, we all have this wisdom written upon our heart, but we don't know how to read it genuinely. The reason for this is simple—we get in our own way because we think we know how our lives should be. Surrendering is largely a process of getting out of our own way so we can live to our highest potential.

Surrendering is the process of realizing the perfection of God in all things. This is not to say that there aren't terrible things in the world, but unbridled hatred of these things will do nothing to remove them. When God asks us to love, He asks us to love everything and everybody, without exception, including ourselves. On the surface level of our reality, things can seem terrible, but, underlying all of that, is God's plan. Saints know this intuitively to be true, and they do their best to live accordingly—step—by step—by step.

Chapter Five

ACCEPT

The second letter in the acronym S.A.I.N.T. is A, which stands for *accept*. At first glance, the word seems similar to surrender, and indeed the two go hand-in-hand. Surrender alone, however, is not enough. Whereas surrender involves an inner shift, a true embracing is acceptance. Acceptance is to let go of all resistance and judgment of the world around you. Through surrender we relinquish our own will and acknowledge the futility of trying to control that which is up to God. Acceptance is your assent to the reality of the situation and is a more outward-bound act of conduct.

If you surrender without 100% acceptance, resistance to God's plan can continue to reside within you. Without the additional process of acceptance, surrender becomes a matter of giving up, like a soldier waving a white flag when he is outnumbered by the enemy. Such a soldier is likely to end up as a prisoner of war. Likewise, surrendering to God without acceptance is another kind of prison. Without acceptance you continue to be confined by the limitations of your own judgments and preconceptions. Only you can look inside and examine if your acceptance is truly genuine.

Sometimes we abuse the word *acceptance* by saying we accept something or someone, when in fact we harbor judgments, resentments, and disapproval. For example, a parent might say, "I accept my son the way he is," but inside he or she may believe the son should be different than he is. What this parent really means is that they have given up trying to change the child, which is a step in the right direction. They have *surrendered* their need to control, but they have not truly *accepted* the child until they have also given up their disapproval. In other words, the parent's love for the child is still conditional, and thus not complete. This failure to accept totally leads to a great deal of conflict within the human psyche. True serenity, however, can only come through full acceptance.

Acceptance is primarily a matter of dropping the fears we carry inside. We tend to think that what is going on inside of us has nothing to do with what we are experiencing on the outside, but this is not the case. Fear is like an invisible poison that affects our relationships with ourselves and others. Fear is at the root of most negative emotions—worry, anger, jealousy, etc. We respond with fear when we feel uncomfortable, and in response the people around us react in fear as well, making the situation even worse. Remaining in a state of acceptance can be difficult in adverse circumstances, but in the end it is the best thing for you and for everyone around you.

An encounter I had with someone a while ago demonstrates the importance of acceptance, what I sometimes refer to as "taking the high ground." I was walking to my car after leaving a deli when I noticed an oddly dressed middle-aged man riding a bicycle toward me. He wore a bandana on his head and carried an acoustic guitar over his shoulder with a large peacock feather fastened to the neck. As he neared me I saw that his bike was a rare vintage model, maybe from the sixties, but in perfect condition. I found this person amusingly unusual, quirky but interesting.

"That's quite a bike you have," I said as he pedaled slowly in front of me.

He offered a broad smile and stopped to dismount, flipping the kickstand to secure his bike. "I have one more like this one in California," he said in a clear British accent. He then twisted his guitar in front of him and immediately stretched his fingers across the fret board of the guitar and began strumming.

"I haven't seen you before," I said, "What is it that you do?"

"I'm a spiritual teacher. I teach Vedic traditions," he answered proudly, looking at me with his wide blue eyes. "I've studied Eastern theology for almost thirty years, and I'm also a chef. I've written a book on specialty meals. I combine my spirituality with cuisine. I love to cook and whenever I teach, I always prepare a nice meal for my students."

I imagined this man to be in his early fifties; his demeanor was quite charming; he was handsome with a childlike face. He embodied a free-spirit personality that I remembered from the "love and peace" movement of the sixties. His polished guitar and fanciful appearance gave him the look of a wandering minstrel. I was curious why this fellow crossed my path at this moment. I, of course, suspected that he was God's choice for me to meet.

"I'm Charles," I said extending my hand.

"Krishna. It's a name I took for myself," he answered with a grin as he puffed up with attitude. "Hey, did you hear about that tsunami in the Indian Ocean? I heard the waves devastated parts of Thailand." Krishna was referring to an underwater earthquake off the west coast of Sumatra, Indonesia, that caused tidal waves that hit the land. Over two hundred thousand people were killed, homes were swept away by the water surge and there were extensive power outages.

"I heard that," I answered. "It sounds pretty bad."

"I can't imagine being there," he said shaking his head. "I've been to Phuket and traveled in that area. It was a paradise."

"The loss of life is always tragic, Krishna," I said, "but even these things are part of God's plan I suppose. My prayers go out to them." We stood silent for a moment.

Krishna nodded approval and shifted his thoughts. "I find Sedona to be a paradise too; awesome scenery, lots of tourists, and quite a mix of spiritual beliefs. But fitting in here has been awkward for me. Most people ignore me because of the flamboyant way I dress. But once they get to know me, they seem to like what I have to say. What do you do?" he asked.

"I live a normal life but I'm open to greater possibilities," I answered. "I accept whomever or whatever comes my way. Each day I ask God to bring people to me and that often leads to interesting situations."

"You trust in God's plan for you," acknowledged Krishna. "And how does that work in Sedona?"

"I don't go out of my way to find Sedona, I wait for Sedona to come to me," I replied. "Something like how you and I are meeting right now. Neither of us had an expectation to meet. We just did. I accept that we're here together for a reason."

"Interesting. You sound surrendered," he said holding his hand to his chin reflecting. "Presuming that God has put us together right now, let me ask you something if I may. I share a flat with some fellows. We share the rent and each have our own space, but today the landlord told me that he's invited his sister and a couple of her friends from Los Angeles to come stay with us. They're going to occupy our common living space. He told me his sister is afraid the disaster in Asia is the beginning of a domino effect of catastrophic events. She's worried that the San Andreas Fault is about to experience a major earthquake. He made his decision without asking the other tenants or me. I'm afraid the other fellows are going to be upset once they hear the news. I'm not sure what I can do."

Krishna was anxious. His tone shifted to one of alarm and I was sympathetic to his concern having unnerved strangers living with him. He confirmed my earlier thought that God had arranged our meeting. I thought for a moment. Then I recalled something a retired military man always told me when we saw each other in town. His words seemed appropriate for Krishna.

"Krishna, you mentioned the tsunami in Thailand and how horrendous it must have been for those who live by the coastline. I see you standing on the beach and about to bear the brunt of crashing waves. This group of visitors who are coming to your house is your tsunami. They're heading right at you and your housemates. What does one do when a giant wave is approaching?" I asked.

"Run like hell!" he exclaimed.

"Something like that. But run to the high ground where it's safe," I told him specifically.

Krishna gave me a curious look, still not certain of what I was suggesting.

"Take a spiritual approach," I explained. "Elevate yourself, Krishna. Rise above the tide of emotions. If you tangle with these people when they're feeling anxious, they'll sweep over you like a giant wave. But if you raise your consciousness to a higher place of acceptance and stay there, then you'll be okay. Accept them in love."

"Yes," mumbled Krishna. "You're right. I have to lift myself above all of this. Good point, Charles. Spoken like a teacher," he said to me reverently, as he folded his hands in a prayer-like gesture. Krishna flashed a bright smile even as the evening darkness fell. It was time for us to go our separate ways. Krishna offered a hug and then mounted his bike and I headed for my car, both of us feeling uplifted by this encounter.

A few weeks later, I saw my minstrel friend on his bike. He pulled up next to me and with a cheerful tone asked, "Charles, how are you?" He climbed off his bike and swung his guitar forward.

"Am I to hear the perfect song?" I chuckled.

"No, but I can tell you the ocean waters are calm!" he blurted back excitedly. "I took your advice, and it's been amazing."

"Tell me . . . what happened with the visitors?" I asked curiously, remembering our first meeting.

"I took to heart what you told me when we last met. It was great advice," he explained glowing. "When they first arrived the energy in the house was tense. The landlord's sister stirred up tensions with her doomsday scenario and had everyone on edge. I shut everything out as best I could. I imagined looking down on the situation from a higher place and acted as though nothing bothered me. My detached attitude seemed to have a calming effect on everyone. I accepted them in love, just like you suggested. As the visitors became more settled, I cooked for them and they loved it. I even played my guitar and got them to sing songs. Things were going so smoothly that after a week the idea of a San Andreas earthquake was forgotten. Several days later the group headed back to Los Angeles. Now there is peace and quiet again."

"That's wonderful!" I replied, seeing joy in Krishna's face. "I'm proud of you for taking the high ground."

"It gets better," he added. "I told you my housemates and I were upset with our landlord. After his sister and her friends left, he apologized to us for his decision to let them stay in the house. He admitted that he overreacted. As a gesture for us being so understanding, he lowered our rent for the month!"

Krishna's experience illustrates the nature of acceptance. Through acceptance, you are instantly transported to a higher perspective, which allows you to see God's view more accurately. His initial reaction was quite normal, given the circumstances—to resist and feel resentment. These situations are indeed like tsunami waves. We can try to swim against them, but how far will that take us? In terms of human emotion, we only add energy to the waves by introducing our negativity into the situation. The group of people he was to encounter was already full of fear, so to have reacted with anger would have been disastrous.

This is not to say that we never stand up for ourselves. It was Krishna's prerogative to make it clear to his landlord that this decision was inconsiderate. The famous "Serenity Prayer" sums up the attitude of acceptance we need in such situations: "God grant me the serenity to accept the things I cannot change, courage to change the things I can, and wisdom to know the difference." With a proper attitude of acceptance, we can view anything that comes into our lives as a gift from God, a chance to develop our wisdom and internal strength.

Acceptance is a form of radical humility. First, you have to have the humility to relinquish your ideas about what God's plan *should* be for you. Whatever you are experiencing and whoever comes into your life are exactly right for you. If you fully accept this precept as true, you will have no problem entering a state of full acceptance.

Secondly, you must have the humility to know that your perspective is limited, that what you perceive of as imperfection is actually part of a bigger picture that you cannot perceive. You can "stand on the high ground" by getting rid of all the ideas of "better than" and "worse than." If you are in a state of true acceptance, it follows that nothing and no one is "unacceptable." A true saint embraces all that is, and seeks to become one with anyone who crosses his or her path.

In this sense, the saint's path is the same as the mystic's path. In all religions, the ones most devoted were the mystics. Regardless of the differences in theology of the different religions, they all sought the same thing: complete oneness with God and all that is. The Christian mystics often referred to this as marriage to God, becoming His yielding bride. The Bible defines the nature of God in very simple terms: "God is love" (1 John 4:8). The poet Rumi, a Sufi mystic, put it this way: "Your task is not to seek for love, but merely to seek and find all the barriers within yourself that you have built against it." Thus, as we break down resistance within ourselves and learn to accept, we allow God (i.e. love) to be present in every situation.

A mystic is someone seeking genuine union with God. It is not about understanding theology or even about having marvelous, transcendent experiences. Rather, mystics seek to step outside of the mind's need to categorize the world into dualities, to label everything as different and separate from self. A mystic lives with conscious awareness of God's presence.

Our lessons in life have nothing to do with shaping the outside world to our liking. Rather, their only legitimate use is inner transformation. Yet too often, we turn our discerning eye upon others and forget about our own internal lives. Christ's teaching on this was very direct:

> Judge not, that you be not judged. For with the judgment you pronounce you will be judged, and with the measure you use it will be measured to you. Why do you seek the speck that is in your brother's eye, but do not notice the log that is in your own eye? Or how can you say to your brother, 'Let me take the speck out of your eye,' when there is the log in your own eye? You hypocrite, first take the log out of your own eye, and then you will see clearly to take the speck out of your brother's eye.
>
> (Matthew 7:2-5)

But don't worry. I'm not asking you to join a monastery or live a hermit's life so that you can contemplate oneness with God in silent bliss. S.A.I.N.T. asks quite the opposite; actually encouraging you to go out into the world, meet with people, and face all of your internal obstacles head on. Hiding yourself away would be too easy because you would never have to face the challenges of the world. The trick is to be "in the world, but not of it" as Christ instructs.

Caroline Myss, an intuitive teacher and healer, uses the phrase "mystical activist" to describe the kind of spiritual interchange I am endorsing. She says:

> You have to look at the person opposite you and think, 'Is this a message or isn't it?' So what are you going to do? You have no option now but to treat that person with the utmost respect. And sometimes it is brutal, but this is an illumination. To illuminate, to bring light to the moment is a mystic in the field. This is true mystical activism.[3] (*Entering the Castle*)

Living in mystical union requires a willingness to erase all illusions of separation between you and other people. The five senses of the body will tell you otherwise—that a person is unworthy, dangerous, unpleasant, etc. To live a saint's life is to see beyond the veil of the three-dimensional world, to realize that the perceptions of the senses

---

[3] Myss, Carolyn. *Entering the Castle*. Audio CD. 2007.

are very limited and that they don't give full essence of the human being in front of you. You must accept the person unconditionally, regardless of circumstances, mental condition, social status, or any other marker of worldly value.

And always remember this—any separation you place between you and the person in front of you is a separation you have placed between yourself and God. As 1 John 4:8 says: "Whoever does not love does not know God, because God is love." Thus, the only measure of God in an interaction is your ability to accept and embrace the other fully.

The time has come for mystics, saints, and sages to come out of hiding and into the world. Perhaps in times gone by there was no point to that because the world was not ready, but now the world is at the brink of transition and mystical wisdom is deeply needed. Consider this poem from Theresa of Avila, a medieval Christian mystic:

> Christ has no body but yours,
> No hands, no feet on earth but yours,
> Yours are the eyes with which He looks
> Compassion on this world.
> Yours are the feet with which He walks
> to do good,
> Yours are the hands with which He
> blesses all the world.
> Yours are the hands, yours are the feet,

Yours are the eyes, you are His body.
Christ has no body now but yours,
No hands, no feet on earth but yours,
Yours are the eyes with which He looks
Compassion on this world.
Christ has no body now on earth but
yours.[4]

Three kinds of acceptance are required: acceptance of self, acceptance of others, and acceptance of God. First, you must accept yourself and the path you have been given. If you don't believe in yourself or don't like something about yourself, you are not accepting yourself as you are. We all have these feelings at times, but really it is a denial of who we actually are. If you believe that you have a divine spirit nature and that God has called you to serve humanity, then there is no need to doubt yourself or your capabilities. Yes, you will be challenged and stumble at times, but understand that all of these moments are perfectly designed for your growth; they are all part of God's greater plan for your life.

Secondly, you must accept other people and everything about the outside world as perfect in God's eyes. S.A.I.N.T. asks you to meet directly

[4]   Vogt, Eric W. /a bilingual edition: *The Complete Poetry of St. Teresa of Avila,* University Press of the South 1996

with others precisely because this is so difficult for human beings, who too often see only from their ego's point of view. The Diary of St. Maria Faustina Powalska, a Catholic saint, reads, "The greater the sinner, the greater right he has to My mercy."

When you are in a true state of acceptance, you will discover that any interaction becomes a "communion of saints" as your divinity steps out from under the mantle of the ego. As you are in the presence of another person in complete acceptance, you will find that they are also able to accept themselves and their situation in that moment.

And last but not least, you must accept God. God accepts you unconditionally, and this is not dependent on anyone else's opinion of you, including your own opinion of yourself. God only cares about the internal, true self that lives within you, not any trappings of success, physical beauty, or any other human measure. All God asks is that we love one another: "Love thy neighbor as thyself." "Do unto others as you would have them do unto you." God is realized through the love that we give one another, so acceptance is the act of opening the "invisible window" and letting God's light shine brightly.

Chapter Six

INVITE

People may avoid the path of S.A.I.N.T. because they do not feel they possess the authority or knowledge to function legitimately as a saint. This may be a legitimate concern. However, relying on others, i.e. priests and gurus etc. to understand life, can short circuit the flow of one's energy. S.A.I.N.T. adopts the premise that wisdom that comes through you is not <u>from</u> you in the sense of your being an individual—a separate entity—walking on earth.

True wisdom does not originate with you. True wisdom can only come through you from a source much greater than yourself. You need not rely on authorities and experts. In fact, the whole notion of "authority" is a construct created by the human ego. If your process of surrender and acceptance is complete and genuine, the next step then is to invite the Holy Spirit as direction. There is no need to be shy or timid because it isn't you anyway; it is the Holy Spirit working through you. After you send out the invitation, what needs to come will come. It is as simple as that.

When you invite the Holy Spirit into a relationship, you have opened the "invisible window." Through the "invisible window" you may peer into what I call the Universal Mind to gain whatever you need in any given situation. The Universal Mind is the sum total of all knowledge, wisdom, and thought and it encompasses all the understanding that mankind has ever achieved and ever will achieve. It includes that which is beyond the human brain to comprehend. It exists in a plane beyond time and space. Ernest Holmes, the founder of the Science of Mind movement, describes it this way: "The Universal Mind contains all knowledge. It is the potential ultimate of all things. To it, all things are possible. It is the unseen plane, the mystery from which all of creation arises."[5] If you have ever had the experience of sudden inspiration, a creativity seemingly coming from nowhere, you probably tapped into the Universal Mind. We tend to think this as an accidental occurrence, but if you surrender to the Holy Spirit, it is like having your own Universal Mind Access Card. Whatever wisdom you need is available to you instantly.

---

5   Holmes, Ernest. *The Science of Mind*. Tarcher, 1928.

The steps of S.A.I.N.T. that precede (3) inviting, the processes of (1) surrendering and (2) accepting, places you in the very center of your inner-self, which is where you need to be, not only to open the "invisible window," but to see through it. Here we look to God for power, wisdom and direction. It is a wonderful serendipity that the letter "I" is in the middle of the word saint. The "eye" that sees through the "invisible window" is the "I" at the center of yourself, the one that transcends the small "I" of the ego. You are in touch with the "I" that lies at the core of your being, your true self, your higher self. This is the "eye" that is capable of seeing through the "invisible window" to the planes that lie beyond the three-dimensional realm. When, from the core of your being, you invite the Holy Spirit into the situation at hand, you unlatch the window and pull it wide open.

Remember, however, that S.A.I.N.T. is not a linear process. You can't expect to walk through these steps like you are walking up the stairs. There is a constant, simultaneous process of reexamination and transformation. One minute you may be in a state of total acceptance, and the next moment the ego sounds the alarm of fear, and you need to return to surrender. This is normal and natural because our minds are bombarded with endless streams of input, some good and some not so good. There is a reason S.A.I.N.T. is called a *practice*—you have to *practice* coming back to the center of yourself over and over until it becomes your habitual state of being.

Giving to others should be the focus of your practice, because this is the way to reveal and subdue the ego. The ego is a master of disguise and it is all too easy to believe we have arrived at a place of spiritual maturity. The ego can even cloak itself in the mantel of spirituality and generosity, so beware of the feelings of superiority that may come with service to others. Understand that The Holy Spirit is not earned, but given entirely by grace.

S.A.I.N.T. awakens your inner "I," allowing you to unconditionally release your love to your neighbor, as you love yourself. God's love shines through you to your fellow man. You may ask yourself, "What will I receive from giving so much of my time and attention to others? Should I expect anything back for myself?" Many of us are taught to think this way, that if we give we should expect something in return. This mind-set will only undermine your best intentions. The Bible says, "It is better to give than to receive." (Acts 20:35) Why is this so? Only by stepping out of our selfish perspective can we invite the Holy Spirit into a given situation.

Who or what is the Holy Spirit? Most people know that He is part of the Trinity of Father, Son, and Holy Spirit, but He is the least understood of the three. The Holy Spirit is the life force of all beings, the living energy that flows through you as you dwell on this earthly planet in your human vessel. It is through God's Spirit within us that we can gain spiritual understanding and insight. The Holy Spirit is eternal, omnipotent and omnipresent. He is referred to as a gift. (Acts 10:45) He can be quenched. (1 Thessalonians 5:19) He is poured out. (Acts 2:17) We are baptized with Him. (Matthew 3:11) He renews us. (Titus 3:5)

The Holy Spirit is the energy that breathes life into man, the birds, the trees, the animals and all of nature's creatures. Within this energy there exists the spirit of God, a holiness that sanctifies life. Embodying the presence of the Holy Spirit is the highest vibration at which human beings can function.

Ultimately, the Holy Spirit is not definable by words or concepts. Nevertheless, everyone holds the desire to feel the Presence of the Holy Spirit; it is the deepest, most persistent longing there is. Any human problem has at its root some blockage to the flow of this Holy Spirit. How will S.A.I.N.T. let you know when the Holy Spirit is present? If your heart and mind remain pure, you will know.

The Holy Spirit is the essence of God permeating the cosmos. The term "Holy Spirit" is the Judeo-Christian term, but He is the *Brahman* of Hinduism, the *Tao* of Taoism, and the *Great Spirit* of Native American religions. All of these names help put the Holy Spirit into human terms, but ultimately they fail to communicate Him. As Lao Tzu writes in the first line of the *Tao Te Ching*, "The Tao that can be named is not the eternal Tao." Likewise, it could be said that "God" as defined by man is not the totality of God.

When Moses asked God for His correct name, He replied, "I am that I am." (Exodus 3:14) This response is as close as we can get to understanding the pure *beingness* of God, and when we get into the center of our own being, into that "I" of our inner core, we are as close as we can get to direct alignment with God. You will know when you have arrived at the center when you are no longer distracted by exterior circumstances. In that moment you are standing right in front of the "invisible window." Invite the Holy Spirit to commune with your essential being and to penetrate the three dimensional reality of your life. Thus the scripture, "The kingdom of Heaven is within you." (Luke 17:21)

I recall meeting someone once during a visit to a local café to buy a cold drink. It was a pleasant day, so I opted to go outside and sit at a familiar table under the shade of a large tree. This round metal table with its four attached seats was occupied by a plainly dressed woman, who appeared to be in her early sixties. She wore a brown blouse and black slacks. A scarf draped over her head. Her dark sunglasses contrasted her light completion; she gave the appearance of someone wanting to be unnoticed. As she was unwrapping a deli sandwich, I asked if I might join her. She gave a lukewarm nod to indicate her approval.

"Thank you," I responded, appreciating her gesture. "I'm Charles."

"Janice," she answered quietly.

"Do you live here, Janice?" asked. "I haven't seen you before."

"I'm from Rhode Island. I live here part time," she replied.

Led by an inner prompt, I said to her directly, "I call this God's table" as I sat down. I often refer to this particular table this way because I have had numerous conversations here about God with friends as well as strangers. It's as though this table incites holiness.

"It looks like an ordinary table to me," Janice said standoffish. She was uncomfortable with my assertion, but she would soon think otherwise, for my words were intentionally directed to awaken her. For several minutes we sat quietly. Janice nibbled one her sandwich and I sipped coffee and watched passersby.

Then Janice broke her silence as she wiped her chin, "I just came from the Mayo Clinic in Scottsdale. I've been taking chemo. It's a struggle to keep yourself together when you have cancer. I wear this scarf because my hair fell out."

"I'm sorry to hear about your condition," I said compassionately. Noticing her need to express her illness, I felt that the Spirit was pulling this out of her.

"Are your treatments helping?" I asked.

"The doctors are taking a wait and see approach," she said unfeeling. "As far as I'm concerned, I'm wasting my time with chemo. We all have to go sometime. I don't really have anything to live for," Janice huffed in a frustrated tone. Her situation seemed unbearable for her. She looked and sounded like a person who had lost all hope.

"Do you have a family or friends for support?" I probed, hoping to shift her thoughts away from herself.

Janice removed her glasses and looked at me with sorrowful eyes. "Not really," she said looking detached. "My husband died four years ago and my children have busy lives of their own back East. A nurse looks in on me, but I have no real friends. I'm on my own." Janice was wrapped in self-pity. Her aliveness was gone.

"What about faith?" I posed hoping to awaken her spirit. "Do you believe in God?"

Janice responded with a troubled sigh, "My faith is gone. I used to believe in God. I was a Christian too. My husband and I attended church together regularly, but after he died, I never felt comfortable going back. I didn't want people to feel sorry for me because I was alone. It was easier for me to avoid church altogether."

Janice had given up on her life. The fear of dying gripped her. Her illness had numbed her ability to love herself or to trust in God. I empathized with situation, however, I recognized her as the person I was to meet, as per my morning prayer. It seemed ironic that she told me she was disconnected from God, while sitting at "God's table."

I felt Spirit at work. "Janice," I said looking at her troubled expression, "remember when I first sat down, and how I called this God's table? I live my life guided by the Holy Spirit. Each morning I ask God to put in front of me the person he chooses for me to meet, that I may serve Him. Right now, this person is you. Maybe we should think of our meeting each other as God's plan for us to share this moment. Maybe there's a bigger plan at work that we don't see."

"I'm not sure what you mean," she asked confused.

"You told me you lost your faith in God. Does that mean God has also abandoned you?" I asked her directly. "Just because you stopped going to church doesn't mean you have to give up on your faith. I know you're going through a tough time, but faith can give you strength."

Janice looked at me with shadowy eyes. Her fingers fidgeted nervously on the table. "I don't hate God," she expressed genuinely. She put her hands to her face to wipe away fresh tears. "I just lost my way," she moaned as her head sank. "I don't feel Him in my life anymore. It's like I have lost all hope in Him. I don't know what to think. I'm scared and I feel so lost."

"Janice, doctors treat the body and make conclusions. They base your chances of recovery on test results. But when you invite the Holy Spirit to come, all things are possible," I suggested.

"What do you mean, Charles? Do you think I have a chance of beating this?"

"One of the main reasons people have faith, is that they believe a chance is possible. Faith is about hope. Wouldn't it be better to place your hope in God?"

Janice folded her arms and leaned back in her seat. "I forgot what hope is," she said quietly. "It's hard to have hope when I'm alone."

"But you are not alone," I said encouraging her further. "Imagine that right now, the Holy Spirit is sitting with us. Right here," I said pointing to the seat next to her. "I have a great sense of peace when I know that He is with me. Janice you can reconnect with God "right now." What better place than here? After all, this is God's table," I asserted confidently.

"I hear you, Charles. But I don't' think God hears me. If He did, where's the proof? 'Right now' as you say, sounds encouraging. But when I'm at home I don't have anyone to encourage me."

I recalled my experience at the cemetery when I, too, wanted proof. I didn't expect a bluebird to fly out of the sky and land on our table, but I did have an unprovoked thought come to me.

"Janice, I just had an intuitive thought," I told her. "The word "listen" came to my mind. Listen for an answer. That will be your proof." I didn't understand what that answer, or proof, might be, but I did recognize Spirit's voice guiding me.

Janice squinted and asked, "Listen to what? I don't hear anything," she said confused.

"I'm not sure, Janice," I admitted. We sat in silence; neither of us knew what to listen for. Suddenly there came a ringing sound. It was her cell phone. Janice reached into her tote bag and answered the call. She turned away from me to talk privately.

"Yes," I heard her repeat several times. "Wow!" she exclaimed surprised. "Okay. I understand," she spoke into her phone. Then she hung up the call.

Janice placed her phone on the table and gave me a huge smile. "It's been a long time since I talked about God with anyone, Charles. I did abandon my faith," she admitted showing regret. Janice sat up in her seat and blew a deep breath. Then she declared with resolve, "I'm going to put my trust in God again. In fact, I believe that's why you're here. I really appreciate you sitting here with me. It's as though we were supposed to meet." Janice showed a remarkable change in her demeanor. Something had dramatically shifted within her.

"I'm glad we were able to share this time together. You seem lighter after your phone call," I said, hoping for an explanation of her change in attitude.

"You said to listen," she answered grinning. "I listened! And I heard!" Janice exclaimed in a bright tone. She offered no further explanation. Instead she glowed with new inspiration; her eyes sparkled with joy. I sensed that Spirit had broken through to her. Maybe it was the phone call, maybe something else. Only she knew. I was content to see her joyful expression and make my own conclusion. Janice and I sat quietly for a few more minutes before we said goodbye. We embraced with a hug.

As Janice departed, she turned to me and said, "I'm going to take a picture of 'God's table' with my cell phone."

"God is close to your heart, Janice."

"I do feel close to God right now," she said appreciatively.

Janice had summoned her own forgiveness for having drifted away from her faith. In final summation, Janice loved God again above all else. She had closed the "invisible window" of her heart, but with only a slight loving nudge from a stranger, she was willing and able to open it again.

Inviting the Holy Spirit into a situation is welcoming the Comforter. Simply unlatch resistance and the "invisible window" opens to allow a grand understanding. Suddenly there is no separation from God and the vastness of His glory.

We humans sometimes pretend to have it all figured out but, in fact, the mysteries of the cosmos are vast and deep, beyond the comprehension of the human mind. Even our most dearly held theologies fail to probe its depth. As Hamlet said to his friend, "There are more things in heaven and earth, Horatio, than are dreamt of in your philosophy." When you invite the Holy Spirit in, you open the "invisible window" to the mystery of all that is, and this allows the essence of God to flow freely through your being.

So much shifts in the human mind when we are able to back up from our usual perspective to see the wider view. This happened in a very literal way as humans ventured into space. The astronauts of the Apollo moon landing all agreed that the most amazing view on the moon was not the lunar landscape, but the sight of the earth rising over the moon's horizon. Seeing the earth from this perspective drove home the interconnectedness and fragility of life, as well as the incredible vastness of the universe. Much later, the Hubble telescope would provide an even more distant image of the earth as nothing more than a pale blue dot floating in the vast darkness of space.

Carl Sagan wrote poignantly of this view of earth:

> From this distant vantage point, the Earth might not seem of any particular interest. But for us, it's different. Consider again that dot. That's here. That's home. That's us. On it everyone you love, everyone you know, everyone you ever heard of, every human being who ever was, lived out their lives. The aggregate of our joy and suffering, thousands of confident religions, ideologies, and economic doctrines, every hunter and forager, every hero and coward, every creator and destroyer of civilization, every king and peasant, every young couple in love, every mother and father, hopeful child, inventor and explorer, every teacher of morals, every corrupt politician, every "superstar," every "supreme leader," every saint and sinner in the history of our species lived there—on a mote of dust suspended in a sunbeam.
>
> The Earth is a very small stage in a vast cosmic arena. Think of the rivers of blood spilled by all those generals

and emperors so that in glory and triumph they could become momentary masters of a fraction of a dot . . . How frequent their misunderstandings, how eager they are to kill one another, how fervent their hatreds. Our posturing, our imagined self-importance, the delusion that we have some privileged position in the universe, are challenged by this point of pale light . . . In our obscurity—in all this vastness—there is no hint that help will come from elsewhere to save us from ourselves. The Earth is the only world known, so far, to harbor life . . . There is perhaps no better demonstration of the folly of human conceits than this distant image of our tiny world. To me, it underscores our responsibility to deal more kindly with one another and to preserve and cherish the pale blue dot, the only home we've ever known.[6]

By surrendering and accepting you may feel like you are an obscure dot, unnoticed and drifting aimlessly. Remember, you are to "be in the world but not of the world." By becoming, as Sagan says,

---

[6] Sagan, Carl. *Pale Blue Dot: A Vision of the Human Future in Space.*

"a mote of dust," is precisely what is needed to move into the core import of S.A.I.N.T. Really, the only way to cope with this seemingly lonely existence is to invite something greater than your small self to come into your reality. You don't need a spaceship to do that; everything is already within you. This allows the inner self of light to shine from within us as a beacon of pure, unadulterated <u>love</u>. The Holy Spirit streams through the "invisible window," as He enters into the realm of human interaction.

Jesus in Matthew 5:16 says, "Let your light shine before men, that they may see your good works, and glorify your Father who is in heaven." Notice that this does not say, "Shine for people, so that they may see the good things you do and praise you because you are so nice." The world is full of empty courtesies and smiling faces that camouflage a selfish heart. These things do not bring harmony and love into the world. You do good, not to receive a reward or even to help another person. You do good, because it is the way the Holy Spirit shines through you to ignite the same in another person. Your soul is a spark of eternal brightness! This must be the light that shines from within you. And as scripture admonishes, (Matthew 5:15) "Don't hide your light under a bushel."

Chapter Seven

NOW

Imagine that you are rowing a small boat through a narrow, winding river. You pass a grove of elm trees and then turn a bend and come upon a field of clover. The elm trees are behind you, in the past, and now, in the present, you are seeing the green clover. But what is around the next bend in the river? You can't see it, it is in the future.

Now suppose that you are flying over the river in an airplane and looking down and see yourself rowing a boat through the river currents. From above you can see the elms, the clover fields and also what lies around the next bend. You see the past, the present and the future all at once. This is how God sees time, as an idea, with no real separation between past, present, and future. Yet, because we are bound by the limitations of our temporal mind, we are also bound by our experience of time.

Time is a phenomenon of the three dimensional world, and S.A.I.N.T. enables you to see a more complete, clearer perception of the flow of time. When you have called on the presence of the Holy Spirit as your guide, the obvious question arises— where am I being guided to? Should I go over that hill? Or that mountain? Do I plan for the future or revisit the past? Actually, the answer is all of these. The Holy Spirit encapsulates all concepts of time into the present moment in our lives—the NOW!

What exactly is the <u>NOW</u>? St. Augustine saw time as a mental construct, so time is the proverbial "zero" designed to give a reference point between events. The "now" seemed to be predicated on the past when the future is anticipated by the "now." Everything that was, is, and will be a "now" is a static point in God's view in the eternal realm. The only things which exist are in the "now." They're really real, really happening, really being. You can't measure what doesn't exist if all that really exists is in the "now." Yet that is exactly what we do with time. Think of each "now" as the self-destructive child of the past that is pregnant with the future.

S.A.I.N.T. regards NOW as the birth moment, the very instance you experience through the Holy Spirit as you peer through the "invisible window." In this instant you are alive with a new consciousness, which plants you in the present moment and all thoughts of the past or future are negated by this new transformation. In this moment you are capable of being in communion with all that exists in front of you in the present. The invitation of the Holy Spirit has awakened you to *present consciousness* where the shade of uncertainty is no longer draped over the "invisible window." It is in the "now" where the Holy Spirit reveals what you are supposed to see, feel, hear or think. Since we are all unique, we will see differently, but the experience is the same—our connection to God. Time freezes. The frame of the moment captures your imagination.

In spiritual circles these days, there has been much talk of the "Now," especially since Elkhart Tolle published his book *The Power of Now*. It has become quite the spiritual buzzword, even touted by Oprah and widely embraced by spiritual teachers.

Tolle is on target when he suggests that staying in the now is the way to end most human suffering. As he explains, most of people's suffering comes from their addiction to mentally focus on the past and/or the future. Never in the present moment, they carelessly fret about the future or relive the hurts of the past. Even war is the result of this addiction, as we carry resentments and expectations to their extremes. The dysfunctions of our personal relationships are just a microcosm of the same failure to remain in the moment.

As a practitioner of S.A.I.N.T., you bring a "State of Presence," the conditioning of being in the now, into your relationship with yourself and others. Staying in the present moment is the only way to keep the "invisible window" open and to peer beyond the limitations of space and time. For a S.A.I.N.T. practitioner, it is impossible to be in the presence of the Holy Spirit without staying in the present. Worrying about the past or future suggests an unwillingness to let go of your need to control. By helping others keep in the moment, both of you will gain access to answers to puzzling questions.

Very often, the people you meet will be haunted by the past or the future. Childhood scarring is a big issue for many people, and fear about the future is almost universal, i.e., personal finances, facing old age, being alone, social trends, etc. By staying present when meeting with others, you help create a safe space for the other person to also stay in the moment. Alan Wilson Watts, one of the first Western Buddhist teachers, described it this way:

> We are living in a culture entirely hypnotized by the illusion of time, in which the so-called present moment is felt as nothing but an infinitesimal hairline between an all-powerfully causative past and an absorbingly important future. We have no present.

Our consciousness is almost completely preoccupied with memory and expectation. We do not realize that there never was, is, nor will be any other experience than present experience. We are therefore out of touch with reality. We confuse the world as talked about, described, and measured with the world which actually is. We are sick with a fascination for the useful tools of names and numbers, symbols, signs, conceptions and ideas. [7]

As a saint, you provide an opportunity to bring the present into relationships brought to you by the Holy Spirit. Usually our personal relationships are sabotaged by fear, which we express through our need to impress or outrank the person in front of us. But you carry with you this simple precept: Eternity exists in the here and NOW. Past and future are nothing more than memory and fabrication. St. Augustine explained it this way: "How can the past and future be, when the past no longer is, and the future is not yet? As for the present, if it were always present and never moved on to become the past, it would not be time, but eternity." [8]

---

[7] Watts, Allen. *The Meaning of Happiness*. Rider, 1978.

[8] Augustine of Hippo. *Confessions*.

NOW is where the shift happens. It is the place in time where true inspiration can be found. True inspiration never happens when our minds are focused on the past or future because these are shaped by fears and preconceptions about what we think we already know. In the present, all those things are stripped away, and we can experience what "really is," not what our memories, opinions, or assumptions tell us is real.

Creative people often mention how their greatest ideas come to them when they are not expecting it—in the car driving, while falling asleep at night, while outside taking a walk. This happens because people have stepped outside of their usual pattern of thinking for a moment. Usually, we look for the answer to problems with an anxious heart, expecting to find the answer in the next moment or the one after that. But really the answer is available right here, right now, and it was always available to us. In the present moment we can see what we know beyond what we *think* we know.

When two people meet, the potential power is even greater. In Matthew (18:20) Jesus says: "For where two or more are come together in My name, there am I among them." I can tell you from innumerable experiences that this statement is true. As a person practicing S.A.I.N.T., you are consciously bringing God into the moment. Yes, the person in front of you must be open and willing to an extent, but in most cases they are brought before you and are at the point of surrender themselves, at least enough to bring inspiration to the issue at hand. After all, would a man walking in the desert refuse drink? You are the Samaritan arriving with a jug of cool water. As Christ said, "I am among you as one who serves." (Luke 22:14)

When this moment happens, when two people meet soul-to-soul in the present, I call this "The Big Bang," referring to cosmologists' theory of how the universe began. In that scientific theory, the universe sprang forth into being essentially out of nothing. Likewise, when you meet a stranger in a loving way, the relationship starts with nothing and love comes from nothing. This is true in the communion of saints as well. Both parties are in a state of nothingness, stripped bare of their egotistical constructs. You, as a practitioner of S.A.I.N.T., have entered this state deliberately, while the other saint has entered this state through the difficulties of life, all of which are perfectly designed to strip us of our pretentions. It doesn't matter if either of you have other egoist issues to deal with in the future. In the moment, right now, both of you are focused on what you have surrendered to God. From this nothingness a vast universe created by love can spring forth, like the explosive expansion that gave birth to our universe. Some great wonders can grow out of nothing, as this story illustrates.

Not long ago I was sitting at a table in a grocery store café talking with friends, an older couple who for twenty-five years owned their own business in Sedona. I enjoyed their warm, happy faces and their New York accents which added a nice touch to the diversity of Sedona. They're great people—funny, kind and loving.

Sarah is the quintessential Jewish mother to everyone she meets—caring, encouraging, and wise. Her husband, Michael, is Greek Orthodox and enjoys sinking his eyes into the New York Times to catch up on the news. He's a bright fellow and a deep thinker, yet he also loves to have fun with people. Both were a delight to chat with.

After we talked for a few minutes, Michael asked me to give him my interpretation of how the Holy Spirit works in me. "How does this happen for you?" he asked curiously in his Brooklyn accent. "Is there some kind of alarm that goes off in your head telling you that the Holy Spirit is present?" Sarah turned away to speak to a passerby as I began to explain to Michael.

"When someone is in front of me," I said, leaning forward toward Michael, "I'm aware of the presence of God in him, and from this point forward a connection between us is established which allows the Holy Spirit to act. The Holy Spirit can speak through me or whoever is in front of me. There is never a set pattern; I'm open to however He comes."

Michael adjusted his glasses. His stoic face reflected that of a wise, contemplative Greek philosopher. With raised bushy eyebrows, and tight lips, it was as though I was speaking with Aristotle. "I'm still not sure how this works," he responded softly. Then in his moment of uncertainty Michael nodded his head toward a middle aged woman who sat alone at a nearby table. She was upset, crying and shaking.

"I tried to speak to her," Michael said in a frustrated tone, "but there's nothing I can do for her. It's a shame to see someone this way." He looked at me shaking his head in dismay. This woman's desperate behavior had upset Michael; he was discouraged even though he'd already offered her assistance.

I glanced at this woman, who sat hunched, with elbows propped on the small round table just five feet away. Her hands hid her face as though she was embarrassed. Behind her stood a shopping cart half full of groceries stuffed into plastic bags. A further look showed me the cashier at the service counter looking concerned. Just then two police officers arrived and confronted this beleaguered woman. A female officer sat at the table and began to question her. This situation was drawing much attention and caused uneasiness within me.

I looked at a despondent Michael who faced me; Sarah peered past her husband at the officers, and I turned my eyes in the same direction. This shaken woman was under much scrutiny. Suddenly, two EMS personnel arrived with a stretcher making this already disturbing problem even more uncomfortable. Whispers erupted all around me, for it appeared that the woman had no money to pay for what she placed in her shopping cart. Her body shook from fear, a medical condition, or both.

This woman appeared agitated as the young police officer pressed for answers, and the cashier looked on helplessly. Store customers stopped to observe, and my friends Michael and Sarah looked on concerned. Sarah shook her head saying compassionately, "This is so sad!"

"Michael," I said looking directly at him to seize the moment, "you asked me how the Holy Spirit works through me. Instead of trying to explain, I'll show you. Please excuse me." I stood up and stepped toward the round table.

"Officer," I said gently, interrupting her as she scribbled a note, "I would like to pay for this woman's groceries. I hope that is okay with you."

The young blonde officer looked up at me with a startled, but consenting look saying, "I suppose that would be all right." I was correct to assume she had no money.

The woman in question began to cry happily, "Oh, thank you so much." Her eyes were shadowy from exhaustion, showing me that this ordeal was too much for her. She looked like a transient—not well dressed, dirty fingernails and hair frazzled.

I walked to the nearby service counter and handed thirty-five dollars to the cashier who smiled brightly. "This is very kind of you," she said relieved of her role in this matter.

In that particular moment I elevated my consciousness to a place of compassion, which others were able to recognize and integrate. A shift occurred. The officer sensed this, as did the troubled woman, and the cashier breathed easy. A conscious awakening was happening. Those who were asleep were now rising and expanding the consciousness of love all around them. Compassion was now sweeping through the café. I returned to the corner table as the petite officer stood up, all five feet two of her.

"You're an angel!" she said, extending her arms to me so I could give her a gentle hug.

This didn't seem like normal police protocol, but her expression of gratitude was being guided by the Holy Spirit. Every action, each gesture, and all who were there were under the direction of Spirit. Onlookers showed loving smiles.

A fellow officer stood nearby; he was six-four and wore a protective armored vest around his wide chest. He directed his stare at me, "I don't suppose you want to hug me?" he asked in a low tone.

"Of course, I will!" I answered with a chuckle. I stood on my tiptoes to wrap my arms around this giant of a man. Laughter erupted from the bystanders behind me who saw me hugging this goliath. Our embrace was amusing but genuine.

By the grace of the Holy Spirit acting through me, this drama was altered. Instead of a predictable outcome, where the wrongdoer is taken into custody and observers feel sad for the occurrence, we found ourselves happy, beaming smiles at one another and acting as our better selves.

The situation calmed as the EMS stabilized a drop in this woman's blood sugar level, the reason for her shaking. She grinned . . . and why not? Her food was paid for, she was being looked after by medics, and there was no further issue with the police. I looked around me. The cashier was going about her business, and the officers were getting warm smiles from citizens. I felt peace and returned to my friends. As I reclaimed my chair with Michael and Sarah, I noticed tears flowing from Michael's eyes and that his wife nodded with her mouth wide open. Sarah looked happily stunned.

"Michael," I said leaning forward, "remember when I told you about connecting a pathway between myself and another so that the Holy Spirit can speak? Well, the Holy Spirit spoke through you, and it was your words that caused me to act. This was the alarm that went off in my head. You were used by the Holy Spirit to cause me to act, so I acted on what you told me."

Sarah beamed lovingly at her husband, her smile filled the café.

Soon the EMS stretcher rolled next to us and the woman, now on her way to the hospital, looked at us and said with a teary face, "God bless you."

"You'll be okay, sweetie," replied Sarah lovingly.

God blessed all of us that day, for in that brief afternoon interlude, those who were present experienced unexpected joy. For a moment we were all one.

Shortly afterwards Sarah and Michael departed for home, while I had one more thing to do; I drove to the hospital to see this woman. I talked with the staff nurses and was told that she was doing well and appreciated the help of strangers. I never saw her again, but at least on that day as her path crossed with our community, she knew she was loved. People felt their oneness and acted accordingly.

Another important part of being in the "now" is learning to act in the "now," just like we all did that day in the grocery store café. The human brain is trained throughout life to always take us out of the present. It is like a nagging parent, asking questions like: Didn't that work out poorly the last time? Are you sure you won't embarrass yourself? What will people think? What will you do when you run out of money? Considering these questions in the back of our minds, we end up abandoning our inner guidance to act. But guidance from the

Holy Spirit comes only in the *now* and must be acted upon in the *now*.

What would Mother Theresa have accomplished if she had said to herself, "Someday I will help those people." Instead she said, "Yesterday is gone. Tomorrow has not yet come. We have only today. Let us begin." Maybe someday inevitably turns into "never" if we let doubt consume our drive to act immediately. Always remember this: being a saint leaves little room for cosmic procrastination.

Does this mean we follow every impulse to act without consideration? No, of course not. The impulse to buy a candy bar or blow a lot of money at a casino is obviously not the same. These impulses come from the body, not from heaven. A good question to ask yourself is, "Does this inspiration come from <u>love</u> or from my own ego?" It can be hard to decipher at times because even philanthropic acts can be motivated by a desire to appear as a "good person" to other people. This is why the process of S.A.I.N.T. is so important as a way to check yourself. There is no time to waste or to be caught up in self-doubt, but you must always check inside to remain centered within yourself. Giving service to others should never require a certain outcome or some reward in return for your actions.

You can never know how, or in what form, inspiration will come. If you expect the direct voice of God, archangels appearing from heaven, or even a visit from a bluebird, you will probably be disappointed. As Benjamin Franklin said in *Poor Richard's Almanac*, "Blessed is he that expects nothing, for he shall never be disappointed." If anything, these inspirations are designed to test your resolve to step outside the box of your own limited thinking. And more often than not, they come in simple, humble ways with no fanfare or recognition.

I remember learning this lesson very clearly one day while driving home in the early morning with a loaf of bread. Suddenly, I had an inspiration to go to a certain church. At first, I felt resistance to the idea for I was on my way home from the store. I was not Catholic and had rarely visited the church. I had no reason to be there and, by earthly standards, I did not belong there. Previously I probably would have dismissed such an idea the minute it entered my head, but I had been practicing S.A.I.N.T. long enough to know not to ignore my feeling. Yet, a voice in my head said emphatically, "Now!" So, I turned my car around, drove to the church and went in.

Inside, a sparsely attended mass was in progress. A burly priest conducted the service. He was older, probably near eighty or more. Suddenly, just as he spoke the words "peace be with you," the priest dropped with a heavy thud to the floor. A lady squealed for help as she ran to his side. The priest lay there in an awkward position in front of the congregation. He needed to be moved. I looked around and realized there was no one to help this man. Everyone in the congregation was older and relatively frail. I quickly realized there was only one person who could help—me. I had hesitated for a moment because all the preconceptions held within my head told me that I didn't belong, that I really should not be participating.

Yes, I did help the priest, and he revived after nothing more serious than a fainting spell. When he came to, I lifted his arm over my shoulder and together we managed to hobble to the cloak room. As he looked into my eyes as though to thank me, I couldn't help but add with a wink, "By the way . . . I'm not Catholic," I said. I learned in that church that we are all called to be of service to each other, and we are not in control of the form that service is meant to take. The important thing is to follow the call of service when it comes, *now*, at the very moment it arrives.

Chapter Eight

TRUST

T he final letter of S.A.I.N.T.—T for Trust— is the foundation upon which the rest stands strong. Through trust, the "invisible window" is propped open and all other aspects of S.A.I.N.T. remain stable.

I remember having a deep experience with trust when I was a young man about to leave for war. I was 23 and found myself in the U.S. Army heading for South Vietnam. I ended up in the Uh Minh forest along the Mekong River, encircled by the largest concentration of regular North Vietnamese forces in country. The recollection of my mother having lost her first husband in war echoed in my mind. All I could do was trust that this tragedy of war would not result in my own demise.

There are times in life when we face death. In this case, I looked my mortality directly in the eye. I carried an M-16 rifle and a grenade launcher, but in truth I knew that if it was my time to go, these weapons could not make a difference. I had to trust in something greater than myself to get me through.

I surrendered the thought of living through that war and made a decision to take it on, one day at a time. A year in a war zone was a lot of days. Trust in a higher power being in charge of my life was all I could imagine and hope for. I had to let go of my family's history in wartime. I saw the scars it left on their lives. This was about survival for me. The war itself was a manifestation of those in power, but soldiers like me had to do the work. We were tasked to see people, the enemy, differently. At a young age, this was a sort of unnatural thinking. Kill or be killed was the mantra. My soul knew this was wrong. Thousands of soldiers and civilians were killed in Vietnam, some I knew personally. Many veterans will agree that the Vietnam conflict was an extension of the military industrial complex, not a war of purpose or meaning. War is the worst emotion of fear, and in the case of Vietnam, it was the dread of those in power who feared losing prestige and grip on the culture. Too often, it is the young and innocent who sacrifice for the fear of others.

But what does it mean to trust? According to the Merriam-Webster dictionary, trust means: "assured reliance on the character, ability, strength, or truth of someone or something." That sounds simple enough, but trust is something far more easily said than done. When we say "I trust you," to another person, it is meant as a pledge of faith in them. Yet, there are times when we intend it as a way of admonishing them not to disappoint us. Likewise, we often proclaim our trust in God, when what we really mean is something like this: "I believe that God will eventually give me what I want."

True trust in God, however, is exactly as the dictionary suggests: "assured reliance" on God. It means that reliance on ourselves and other people is secondary to reliance on God. When we trust God completely, we are able to stand down to let God direct the situation. The Holy Spirit is ready and available to come flowing through the "invisible window" as pure, unadulterated grace into any human situation. We need only get out of the way through trust.

In many ways, life is like standing with your nose pressed up against a Rembrandt painting. All you would see from that close-up perspective is a crazy assortment of bold brushstrokes, some bright and cheerful, others gray and gloomy. The same is true for our lives. God is the great Artist and only He sees the big picture. The events of our lives are the brushstrokes that make up the totality of life's composition. If you can back up a bit from the "right" or "wrong" of the situation, you will be able to sense the presence of a Master at work. Trust is an acknowledgement that we are not the ones who ultimately decide the content of our lives, but through trust we can become active co-creators in the process.

I remember once encountering a man who was lacking in trust, who felt disabled by his financial worries. He was a gifted jewelry craftsman who sold his pieces independently and at craft fairs, but recently he had a hard time selling any of his works. The pieces sold for about $40 apiece, and this was too much of a luxury for most people during a time of economic downturn. The man was now worried that he could not pay rent or even feed himself if it continued like this.

Intuitively, I felt that his own lack of trust was blocking the flow of money more than anything, so I said to him, "I have an experiment for you to try. Are you willing?"

"I don't know. What do I have to do?"

"Just trust," I replied.

"Trust what?"

"Do you believe in the Holy Spirit?"

"Yeah . . . I guess," he answered.

"Trust that the Holy Spirit will provide what you need."

The man thought about it for a while, but not seeing many other choices, he finally relented and said, "Okay."

"The next time someone comes up to look at the jewelry," I instructed, "don't say a price. Just tell them to pay what they feel it's worth."

At first, the thought worried the man a bit. The stones alone were worth a lot, so it seemed like a big risk. But finally I could see him relax into the idea.

Within a few moments, a woman came up to the table we were sitting at and began to look at the jewelry and complimented his work. She picked up a stunning necklace and admired it closely. "How much is this one?" she asked.

"I'll give it to you for whatever you think it is worth," he replied.

She thought about it for a moment, glanced in her pocketbook, and said, "Is $80 enough?"

"Certainly," he replied with a grin, as she set down four twenties on the table.

A few moments later, the scene repeated itself as another lady offered $60 for a piece. My friend was amazed. "I can't believe it," he said smiling.

"Actually, you did believe it, at least for the moment, and that's the key. You let the Holy Spirit be present by letting go of your worries," I replied.

In this case, the man got what he needed by choosing to trust for a moment. The caveat here is that trust does not always get us what we think we want. Rather, it will deliver precisely what we need. In this case the man had a simple need for money to cover rent. It could have turned out a completely different way. If he had needed a simple lesson in generosity, perhaps the women would have only offered ten or $20 dollars, maybe not even enough to cover the cost of his materials. Trust is easy when what we want is delivered like presents from Santa Claus, but this is not to our greater benefit, because it is the unfortunate nature of the human to learn greater character through hardship, not ease.

Even if there is a tangible reward, you must stay true to your inner guidance. If you follow the other steps of S.A.I.N.T. and practice them diligently, you will learn to hear this inner voice very accurately. This is the part of you connected directly to God, the part through which God alerts you with a small, calm inner voice of guidance.

To remind yourself of trust, the part of you that trusts unconditionally, you may want to think of the image of the cross. Conveniently, the word *trust* begins and ends with the letter T, which is in the shape of the cross. In Christianity, the cross is, of course, the symbol of Christ's crucifixion and resurrection. This is apropos for the follower of S.A.I.N.T. because Christ's sacrifice on the cross is symbolic of the continual death and resurrection process we all must embody.

Significantly, the image of the cross has meaning across many cultures and through many eras. The ancient Egyptians, for example, used the cross as a hieroglyphic meaning "life" or "living." In Hinduism, the vertical shaft represents the higher, celestial states of being; the horizontal bar represents the lower, earthly states. In other words, the cross represents the conjunction of heavenly and earthly concerns, which is exactly the purpose of S.A.I.N.T.

The cross is also associated with the number ten, which, in our numbering system, is the number of completion since it is based on tens. In Chinese calligraphy, the cross is the symbol for ten, and in the Roman numeral system, this is turned on its side to form an X. You can still see the X added to the cross in Catholic tradition, especially in the context of the Vatican. X is also the first letter of the Greek word for Christ, thus we use Xmas in place of the longer Christmas. The completion of humanity's purpose can only be accomplished when the will of God is rectified with the will of Man.

True trust means having the faith that all things have their purpose within God's plan, even if they are not to our liking in the moment. Undoubtedly, there will be moments in your life when trust is pushed to the absolute limit. The rational, human mind will shout, "Why are you doing this, God?" You must not follow the ranting of this voice, but instead listen to the quiet inner voice that whispers, "Trust . . . trust . . . trust." If you are in touch with your highest self, you will hear this voice, and through the practice of S.A.I.N.T. you will learn that this is the only guidance worth following. All other "sensible" opinions have little meaning by comparison.

I vividly recall an occasion when my trust was pushed to the extreme. It was early morning, just before sunrise, and my wife had just left for work. She drove her car as usual.

Minutes after she left the house, the phone rang. I heard a strange woman's voice speaking, "Your wife was in an accident. I'm with her. Please come right away."

Her words seemed surreal. My heart sank. "This can't be happening," I thought. I grabbed my car keys and raced to the scene of the accident. An ambulance had already arrived. Flashing lights from two police cars, eerily lit up the dark roadway, and showed my wife's car stopped in the intersection. The front end of her car was crumpled and the driver's side door was open, exposing an inflated air bag. I didn't see my wife. Another wrecked automobile sat idle on the curb. I did not expect to see so much damage. Both cars appeared to be totaled. A sense of panic set in. "Where is my wife? Is she hurt?" I wondered frantically. I needed to calm myself.

As I stepped out of my car I took a deep breath and quietly whispered the words of S.A.I.N.T.— *surrender, accept, now, invite,* and *trust.* I closed my eyes and repeated the words three more times. I needed to shift my consciousness before I faced whatever circumstances might be presented to me. As I walked toward the accident scene I blurted out, "trust . . . trust."

Suddenly I felt calm, an inner peace filled me. My fear subsided. In a state of surrender I approached the parked ambulance. The back doors were flung wide open. I looked inside and saw my wife sitting upright on a side bench, trembling. She was alive! Two paramedics were comforting her. A great relief came over me. My wife was shaking and crying but appeared unhurt.

Overjoyed with gratitude, I calmly reached for her hand. We were together again! Our eyes locked in a loving gaze, as though we were just reunited after a long separation. What were only passing minutes, seemed like hours to me. Now time stood still. My prayer had been answered and my wife was okay. Remarkably the other vehicle's driver was also not injured. The experience was highly emotional for me, but the outcome was miraculous!

The power of S.A.I.N.T. is putting "trust" into practice, by making it such a powerful theme in your life that you view every event, every sorrow, every prayer with the unshakeable conviction that is God totally, spotlessly trustworthy. These moments are actually great blessings in disguise, because they will both test and expand the limits of your ability to trust. You cannot know the strength of your trust until you are tested. In any crisis we are at the mercy of whatever outcome may unfold. We must "let go and let God" in order to lift the burden from ourselves. The pressure's off you and on God, and He can handle it perfectly.

In Romans 8:28 Paul says, "And we know that all things work together for good to them that love God, to them who are called according to his purpose." I began my path confronted by my own doubts. Yet, when I allowed myself to follow my inner guidance, I found myself being used as a tool of God's grace that I could not have possibly orchestrated through my own will. There was one event that illustrates how a miraculous combination of situations can all come together in service of God.

After I experienced my inner awakening at the cemetery I was not sure of what to expect next, if anything at all. Every day I would visit the cemetery and stand before the statue of Mother Mary. I waited and hoped for something to inspire me. Days went by and nothing extraordinary happened. I grew discouraged and was ready abandon the notion that I might live more fully in the spirit.

On a particular visit, as I stood before Mary's statue, I needed to speak. "Mary, I'm not sure of what to do. I feel discouraged. I come here and pray and feel there's more that I can do, but I'm not sure of what that is. Am I supposed to help others? I need your direction."

I placed my hand on Mary's weathered stone shoulder and felt warmth. Sunlight covered her statue and danced around us. Suddenly my inner voice spoke to me . . . *Ask him about his brother.* I jerked my hand away from Mary as though it were she who had spoken to me. Those unprovoked words startled me and I was confused. I didn't know where the words came from. Then they repeated a second time . . . *Ask him about is brother.* I looked into Mary's eyes. They appeared to be authentic for an instant, perhaps enlivened by the reflective sunlight. I stepped away and faced the many gravestones, remembering the bluebird. "Could this be another sign for me?" I wondered.

The words seemed instructional. I was to ask someone about his brother, but to whom did this refer and where would this question lead me? I had no experience interpreting such thoughts. Should I act on a thought? Perhaps this was how I was to trust my new found faith. I waited, hoping that I might get clarity. Minutes went by and nothing followed.

Shortly thereafter, I left the cemetery and walked down the asphalt driveway to the main road. As I neared the bottom of the hill I noticed a rugged man clearing brush. He wore coveralls, appeared to be in his forties and he held a small saw. My thought was to confront this man and ask him if he has a brother. But this seemed too risky. This would mean that I was following a voice and trusting in something other than my own logic. I could have appeared foolish if I was not careful of what I said. And the question about a brother was all I had to ask. I had no further explanation beyond the question itself. However, if I was to allow myself to be guided, I needed to act. I chose to be cautious.

I decided to call this man from a distance. If he didn't respond favorably, I could always say I mistook him for someone else. My courage was lukewarm.

"How's your brother?" I shouted from thirty yards away. My voice echoed in the morning silence and I got his attention. He paused for a moment and looked in my direction, as if he might know me, but then resumed his work. We made no connection. My question was misdirected, so I turned onto the main road and walked home.

The inner words that came to me at the cemetery continued to puzzle me for another day before I let them go. I didn't have an explanation.

It was several days later when I returned to the cemetery. I noticed the same man clearing the thicket. He noticed me as well, however, this time he called out to me.

I immediately recalled my asking him about his brother. Could I have misread our first encounter? I wondered why he wanted to speak to me. We met at the clearing's edge.

"I'm Steve. The other day I thought I heard you mention my brother. Do I know you?" he asked politely. Steve was a rough looking man but had a soft spoken voice.

"I'm Charles," I said hastily. "Yes, I remember calling to you. I must have mistaken you for someone else. I'm sorry for the confusion."

Steve had more to say. "I have a brother and when I heard you call, I thought you might know him. He's been on my mind a lot."

I felt an unseen presence around us. It was the same feeling I had when I stood by Mother Mary's statue. I was now comfortable being with Steve. He seemed sincere and I sensed he wanted to tell me more about his brother. So I asked, "Where is your brother? Does he live around here?"

"No, he lives in Kenosha. Not too close. Right now he's in the hospital dealing with health issues. I guess that's why I reacted to your question. I'm worried about him."

"Not too serious, I hope?" I replied with concern. Steve lowered his head and his demeanor saddened. I perceived this health issue to be very serious.

"My older brother, Phil, is in intensive care," Steve informed me. "He's been in the hospital for some time and it doesn't look too good. He needs a liver transplant. It's been touch and go for him."

Hearing him say the word "brother" seemed uncanny. Perhaps this <u>was</u> the man I sought. I was struck by Steve's openness. He expressed his heartfelt emotions to me, a stranger, yet, it was as though he felt compelled to speak. I was being guided by a strange force. I was supposed to be there.

"I'm sorry to hear that he's not well," I offered compassionately. "It sounds like your brother needs a miracle." A curious choice of words for me to use, I thought.

"I'm afraid it will take a miracle, but I still have hope," Steve replied. "My brother can't survive without a new liver. He's been on a waiting list."

"This sounds serious, Steve. I can understand your concern. I've heard about donor waiting lists. Doesn't someone have to pass away in order to receive a liver?" I asked.

"That's how it works," Steve confirmed. "Once a donor has been identified, the organ is delivered to the hospital for the transplant. But no one ever knows when that can happen. That's the hard part. The waiting and hoping."

I tried to imagine such a scenario. The donor process is a dichotomy. Someone has to lose their life in order that another may live. Sadness for the deceased's family yet joy for the recipient. I left this thought and concerned myself with trying to comfort Steve. But first I needed to speak openly with him as he had with me.

"Let me share something with you, Steve. I told you earlier that I mistook you for someone else, but in fact, I really wasn't sure what I was saying the other day," I confessed. "This may seem odd, but I feel I should tell you everything that transpired."

"I don't understand," Steve questioned.

I began to explain. "I don't know you or your brother, but the day when I first saw you might have been predetermined. If this sounds strange, it's because it is. I'll tell you what I was feeling. While you were here clearing brush, I was at the cemetery standing by the statue of Mary. Not long ago I had an unusual experience there. I call it my epiphany. Somehow I came to know God, and ever since that day I've had unusual feelings. I'll describe it as having the Holy Spirit being in my thoughts. Like an inner voice speaking to me." Steve squinted when I mentioned the Holy Spirit. I continued.

"Just before I saw you, this inner voice spoke to me as I was standing next to the statue of Mary. I was asking her for direction and these words came to my mind . . . *Ask him about his brother.* I didn't know what to think."

Now Steve listened intently. Something I said stirred him.

"Steve, I've only felt spiritual for a short time. I haven't been able to understand what I'm supposed to do, but I do feel called. So when these words came to me, I assumed I would find someone who has a brother and ask, just as I did with you. I just don't know what it means."

Steve put his hand to his chin, thinking deeply and then spoke. "I've seen the statue. It's in the old Catholic cemetery. That's quite a place up there," he said nodding his head. "I'm glad you came to know God, however that happened. Sometimes when we're called it's just to follow our instincts. It sounds like this is what you're doing. You got me thinking when you said this so tell me more about this voice you heard."

I appreciated that Steve allowed me to speak honestly. "This voice was more like a thought that came to my mind," I explained. "These words were clear but I haven't heard anything else. I called to you thinking that you might be the one I was to ask about a brother. But since we didn't connect the other day, I let it go. Now here we are talking about your brother. Does this make any sense?"

"Maybe," replied Steve. "The voice might have been a sign. Maybe for you and me. I'm a Christian, Charles, and I believe these things are possible. You might be a messenger."

"I'm not suggesting that I know anything, Steve. However, I feel that God has brought us together for a reason. I know this all sounds a bit strange, but my experiences at the cemetery have been even stranger. I'm not sure what to make of this. Maybe you have an idea?"

Steve rubbed his eyes and looked up at the sky. After a pause he took a deep breath and sighed. "I'm not sure either," he said. "I do believe that God sometimes uses us for different reasons. I trust what you said. Your words have me thinking about Phil. He needs all the help he can get. If I might ask, tell me what you feel about his chances of making it. Do you feel anything inside? Like a gut instinct?"

Steve asked me to draw on my intuition and I wondered if I should answer him. I opened myself to feel if spirit was guiding me. Something came to mind. I imagined seeing two men standing together. Perhaps it was Steve and Phil. I couldn't be certain. I felt no resistance, so I answered him.

"Steve, I think your brother is going to be okay. I have no evidence of this to be true. It's just what I feel and I do feel strongly about this. Let's hope I'm right."

"I won't hold you to it, Charles. I do appreciate your opinion. There's something about your confidence that makes me want to think you're right." Steve perceived the Holy Spirit acting through me.

"I feel my epiphany was a miracle for me," I said. "I never expected to be blessed by such an experience. Why shouldn't you expect a miracle for your brother?" Spirit had encouraged me to plant a seed for something miraculous to happen.

"Miracle is a beautiful word," Steve sighed hopefully. "I appreciate your thoughts, Charles. I've been asking God for a sign. I wanted something to instill hope in me about my brother. Phil's wife and our family pray every day for a miracle. It can't be a coincidence that you and I are talking."

Steve made me realize that I was being used as a vessel for Spirit. I could only hope this to be true and that I was worthy. We soon departed and went our separate ways.

I continued to visit the cemetery regularly but I did not see Steve. Three months went by before our paths crossed again. Something special awaited me. I was driving my car on the same country road where Steve and I first met, when I noticed two men standing together near the clearing. One man was wearing familiar coveralls. I slowed down for a better look. It was Steve. I stopped my car and stepped out to say hello.

"It's been a long time, Steve," I said, greeting him with a smile.

"Charles, it's great to see you!" he exclaimed happily surprised. "I was hoping I would see you again. Perfect timing! I want you to meet someone."

The other man approached. He was tall and thin, somewhat fragile. "This is my brother, Phil," introduced Steve proudly. Phil provided a huge smile.

I was stunned! Steve's eyes glistened with tears of joy and I, too, had a lump in my throat.

I shook Phil's hand. His grip was weak but sincere. As I looked into Phil's cavernous eyes he seemed grateful. His unshaved face showed humility.

"I'm glad you pulled through, Phil," I said warmly.

"I received a lot of prayers," he replied graciously. "I'm a walking miracle! Thanks for being a part of this," Phil said appreciatively. "Steve told me all about how you two met each other."

"It was God's plan, Phil," I declared. Steve gave a nod of agreement.

The three of us shared our time together grateful for Phil's "miracle" recovery.

Meeting Steve and his brother was a special experience for me. What began with my concern for my own spiritual well-being ended with my being introduced to a man and his brother whose life's struggles were far beyond what I experience in my own life. Yet, they were children of God whom God chose for me to meet, appreciate and love. By opening up to Spirit and trusting in God's will, the heart opens wide.

If you find yourself doubting, forgive yourself. This is part of the journey and part of learning to trust yourself. But each time you return to TRUST, you will find your capacity to do so open to the Holy Spirit.

In most difficult times I remember this verse: "Be still and know that I am God." (Psalm 46:10) God asks very little of us beyond this—the simple state of being open to the world of spirit.

Chapter Nine

GOING FORTH

Mother Theresa called us to inner awakening, "Holiness is not a luxury of a few. It is everyone's duty: yours and mine," she said. I am suggesting that when you practice S.A.I.N.T. you live inside the view that lends significance to even the most ordinary interactions. This allows you to let go of separation identity. You awaken to greater consciousness. Connecting in oneness opens you to revelation. As God's children, we have the Universal Mind of God available to us. We have access to our Universal Mind for ideas and inspiration, and it is through this Creator, God, that all things are possible.

The "invisible window" puts this new vision right before you. You only need to peer through to see clarity. You may have a curtain draped over your heart, a shade pulled over your inner window, but the practice of S.A.I.N.T. can guide you. Lift the veil and reveal God's light.

As you go out in the world to live your life as a saint, try to remember that this practice exists as a process of purification. Some things you experience will be easy and some things will be difficult. Either way, you must trust that all of these things are perfectly orchestrated for your own growth. S.A.I.N.T. is only there to help you go back into yourself again and again, just as you need to clean your house again and again to keep it clean. With time, however, all these things will become a normal and natural part of life, a "S.A.I.N.T. reflex," of sorts. By embracing the pillars of S.A.I.N.T., you are one step closer to your own inner freedom.

Don't be discouraged that S.A.I.N.T. is not a linear path. This practice is meant to draw you away from observing the spiritual experience from the sidelines. Jesus gives clarity in Luke 17:20-21: "The kingdom of God does not come with your careful observation, nor will people say, 'Here it is,' or 'There it is,' because the kingdom of God is within you."

Buddhists describe the process of enlightenment as "dying before you die" because you have to give up so much of who you *think* you are. Jesus also asks for a death to one's ego self, as He demonstrated on the cross. Too often we have shifted responsibility for dying to self away from ourselves, thinking we can be "saved" by attending church and professing "right beliefs." I am asking you, through S.A.I.N.T., to walk your talk in a more real way than that. Christian writer A.W. Tozer stated it this way: "Among the plastic saints of our times, Jesus has to do all the dying, and all we want to hear is another sermon about His dying." I am asking you to become a real-in-the-flesh saint, right here and right now!

Of course, you don't have to sit in a monastery while waiting for the Holy Spirit to arrive. You can go about your day and pursue your goals as usual. However, from this moment on, there lies within you a knowing, an awareness, that there is a greater plan beyond your own. There need not be any striving or anxiety in the pursuit of the Holy Spirit. Merely be receptive to the gift.

Try to remember the acronym S.A.I.N.T. in times of trouble to bring you back to your center. Think of surrender and trust as two mighty pillars holding up the S.A.I.N.T. practice like columns on a great cathedral and then always come back to the "I" within yourself, inviting the Holy Spirit into your communion with other saints.

Above all, remain patient with yourself and treat yourself with the respect a saint deserves. Peace within your mind and heart is far more important than something happening out there in the world. When you pray for God to bring you the circumstances He has prepared for you, there may be a time of waiting without direct perception of the Holy Spirit. As Psalm 37:7 says, "Be still before the Lord and patiently wait for Him."

Our culture engenders impatience in us, a desire for instant gratification. Even in spirituality, we take a results-oriented position, thinking that any effort is wasted if it does not have tangible results in the material world. The greatest gifts we receive are always internal, not external in nature. If it is time to <u>wait</u>, this is precisely the right thing to do in the moment. If we have to <u>act</u>, then this is also the right thing to do in the moment. The point of S.A.I.N.T. is to make every moment sacred, thus cultivating and drawing out the highest version of ourselves.

When I first experienced my awakening, I was simply out for a jog; I was not in any sort of deep spiritual contemplation, certainly not expecting anything spiritual to happen! Yet I arrived at the place and time prepared for me. I stood before a statue of the Blessed Mother Mary and asked for a sign from God, a sign that would leave no doubt in my mind. Without knowing it, I invited the Holy Spirit to arrive. And then it happened, out of the blue. Standing there in a cemetery, I was suddenly filled with a love beyond anything I had ever felt. The Holy Spirit was able to break through the facades I had built up through my lifetime. There was no reason to think I deserved this, yet by simply asking in a moment of surrender, an "invisible window" opened into my heart.

Since that time in the cemetery, my experience of the Holy Spirit has run the gamut between ordinary to extraordinary. I, like you, have to pay bills and get chores done. There is nothing about living one's sainthood that takes you away from the ordinary things of life. The difference is in the knowing, and the recognition that the Holy Spirit is always there beyond the "invisible window," ready to flow in once again.

At times you will wonder why you have been asked to meet certain people, those who have been put before you. Some will be resistant and even scoff at you. This, yet again, is perfection in action, as difficult as it may seem. You are not a saint because you want or deserve glory in this world. If the world gives you the exact opposite, then you have been given the chance to examine and clarify your motivations on your path. Allow the Holy Spirit to assist you and every once in a while, you may see someone blossom right before your eyes. That will be a gift indeed.

If your path ever seems difficult or lonely, I would ask you to think of the world as a manifestation of the kingdom of heaven. To whatever degree the world fails to live up to that label, it is merely the result of our disconnection from God. Having a particular result here on the earthly plane is not the goal of this practice, yet inevitably you will reduce suffering in the world if you practice sincerely. First and foremost, you will eliminate your own suffering, since all suffering comes from resistance to God's plan for you. Along the way to that realization, you will very likely ease the suffering of others in this world as you show them compassion and offer them your insights.

The practice of S.A.I.N.T. is not about saving the world, since it is merely a temporary illusion anyway. Nevertheless, I believe you do have the potential to make this world a better place. Even if this world is a temporary condition, why not make it a more harmonious place while you are here?

S.A.I.N.T. is a "pay it forward" practice. While the purpose is for your personal, inner growth, it is meant to have physical manifestation as well. Meeting with others is essential because staying by yourself is far too safe. Your saintliness must be challenged and practiced to be refined.

As you perfect S.A.I.N.T. within yourself, it will inspire the same in the people you meet. As you perfect the practice of keeping within the center of your higher, saintly self, others will naturally drop their defenses and open up to God, just as you have. Can you imagine how different the world would be if everyone were to serve each other in this way?

When you meet another person with the assumption that he or she too is a saint, you have the opportunity to light a candle within another soul. And that person in turn has the opportunity to do the same with others. The long term results of your saintly actions are, in this sense, beyond your comprehension.

There will be naysayers and skeptics who will criticize and mock you. Yet to be called a "buffoon of God," as was St. Francis of Assisi, offers a chance to be grateful for a little suffering. St. Francis believed that we are somehow connected to everything as brothers and sisters—the moon, the sun, the trees, the birds and animals, to each other and even brother death. As St. Francis said, "God wanted me to be a new kind of fool in the world." If you are meant to be a fool, too, then go forth and be a fool!

My own experience of interacting with the bluebird was indeed my "St. Francis moment," for I did truly connect with a brother creature of nature in a beautiful and profound way. At that instant, I realized what a silly buffoon I had been before God and how my idea of separation was just an illusion that kept me from self-discovery. The "invisible window" had flung wide open for me. Going forth, I would shine my light as a "new kind of fool" in this world.

Finally, think of S.A.I.N.T. as a way back to the Garden of Eden. In the Biblical story, Adam and Eve were cast out of the garden for eating of the fruit of the Tree of Knowledge of Good and Evil. This is symbolic of our human tendency to believe we know something, that we can delineate and cast out all that is "bad" or "wrong" about the world on our own terms. S.A.I.N.T. encourages you instead to embrace all the circumstances that you experience as divine gifts from God. In doing so, the "invisible window" is thrown open and the fresh air of the Holy Spirit's "garden" flows through our hearts again.

S.A.I.N.T. AFFIRMATION

S.A.I.N.T. is a practice affirming love and compassion to yourself and to others. To affirm something means to make it firm, to give it shape and substance and permanence. As a saint you are projecting a *strong, positive, feeling-rich behavior that is genuine.*

The five principles of S.A.I.N.T are clear and concise. <u>Surrender</u>, <u>accept</u>, <u>invite</u>, <u>now</u> and <u>trust,</u> are specifically meant to assist your transition to live more fully in the spirit. Limiting the practice to only five principles, helps to keep your process of transformation achievable. It is essential that you invoke all five of them together. Otherwise, you will negate the strength of the practice. To quote Aristotle, "The whole is greater than the sum of its parts." The S.A.I.N.T. practice requires the full integration of all five principles.

Here are examples of strong, positive S.A.I.N.T. affirmations:

> "I completely surrender to God's plan for me."
>
> "I totally accept God's will."
>
> "I willingly invite a Higher Power to comfort, teach and guide me."
>
> "I am present to God's revelation and glory."
>
> "I faithfully trust that Divine love is guiding me."

Below are guidelines you may want to consider for your practice.

1. Always express your affirmations in the present tense. For example: "I am a saint." Avoid using future tense, for example: "I am going to be a saint."

2. State affirmations positively. You might say, "I surrender to God's divine will" rather than "I do not have spiritual aspirations."

3. Make you affirmations short and specific. The S.A.I.N.T acronym consists of five "one word" principles—surrender, accept, invite, now and trust.

4. State you affirmations in the 1st person. To live more fully in the spirit you must "own" your practice. Say "I trust" for example.

5. Make S.A.I.N.T. real to you. Saintly behavior requires your conscious attention and action. Being present in all situations will keep you aware. Full awareness will make your practice real to you.

6. Commit to your practice with determination. Dedicate yourself to live more fully in the spirit. Your commitment will reap immense rewards.

7. Stay within the boundaries of the practice. A good golfer keeps his golf ball in the center of the fairway. He avoids the rough. A lapse in your focus can cause you to stray off course. Avoid the weeds. Stay centered.

8. S.A.I.N.T. is a process of spiritual growth. Be comfortable and allow yourself to settle into the practice at your own pace. This is not a race or a competition. Your growth will come in relation to the effort you apply to the practice.

A SAINT'S RESPONSE

Life tests our behavioral responses in many ways. Disappointment, rejection, or falling short of an expectation, these can all lead to a sense of unworthiness. Being a saint does not mean that you will not have a "bad result," or a "bad day." But you are never unworthy. Remember, your spirit cannot be tarnished in any way. You are an eternal being. Even in the darkest times, our spirit rises above the superficial.

Allow the Holy Spirit to be your guide; surrender to His Higher Power. A saint is wiser and smarter than his conscious mind and he is less confused by emotions or complexity. Trust that you will arrive at correct conclusions or responses.

The contention between volatile emotions and a calm response is illustrated below.

Genuine Emotion	A Saint's Response
Resentment	Honesty
Frustration	Patience
Jealousy	Self-Love
Stubbornness	Relaxed acceptance
Fear	Comfort
Sorrow	Compassion
Greed	Generosity
Doubt	Trust
Anxiety	Surrender
Denial	Simple Presence (Now)
Self-hatred	Wholeness
Desire	Giving
Temper	Embrace obstacles
Self-importance	Humility
Loneliness	Faith
Confusion	Prayer
Rejection	Contentment

NOTES

NOTES

NOTES

NOTES